BlackStone's Gambit
Orchestrating a Global Takeover

Written by:
Alan E Shields

INDEX

Chapter 4 35

The Woke Ideology: A Mask for Manipulation 35

Chapter 5 45

The Energy Crisis Conundrum: A Calculated Play.....................45

Chapter 6 56

The Chinese Connection: A Dance with the Dragon..................56

Chapter 10 100

The Political Weave: Manipulating the Strings of Power 100

Chapter 11 111

The Non-Profit Nexus: Benevolence or Ulterior Motives? 111

Chapter 12 123

The Global Resonance: The Final Note in BlackStone's Symphony of Control 123

Chapter 1
The Financial Maestros

The Puppet Masters of Global Finance

In the intricate maze of the global financial landscape, where corporations and conglomerates jostle for supremacy, BlackStone stands apart. Their presence isn't just felt; it's overpowering. Every move they make sends ripples through stock markets, every decision they take influences economies, and every strategy they deploy sets the tone for other players. They don't just participate in the game; they dictate its rules.

Nestled in the shadows, yet exerting an influence that's impossible to ignore, is their silent partner, GlobeGuard. A formidable entity in its own right, GlobeGuard's alliance with BlackStone amplifies their combined might. Together, they don't merely navigate the turbulent waters of global finance; they create the storms and then offer the umbrellas. Their synergy is a masterclass in strategy, with BlackStone's overt moves complemented by GlobeGuard's covert operations.

In the dimly lit boardroom of BlackStone's headquarters, executives gather around a massive table. Charts, graphs, and numbers flash across screens, but the atmosphere is calm, almost eerily so. "Gentlemen," begins the CEO, his voice dripping with confidence, "our next move will not just shake the markets; it will reshape them." Murmurs of agreement fill the room, but everyone's attention is on a single empty chair at the head of the table. It's reserved for a representative from GlobeGuard, who never attends in person but whose presence is always palpably felt.

A screen flickers to life, and a distorted voice fills the room, "BlackStone, our plans are aligned. The world thinks it's free, but every string they dance to is held by us." The room goes silent, absorbing the weight of the statement. The alliance between BlackStone and GlobeGuard isn't just about financial dominance; it's about control, influence, and a shared vision of a world where their reign is unchallenged.

As the meeting concludes, the executives disperse, each carrying out their part in a grand plan. They know they're not just making business decisions; they're shaping the future. And in this future, BlackStone and GlobeGuard don't just play the game; they own it.

Beyond Profits: A Quest for Absolute Control

In the sprawling metropolis of New York City, atop one of its gleaming skyscrapers, lies the opulent headquarters of BlackStone. The building itself is an architectural marvel, but it's not its height or grandeur that sets it apart; it's the aura of power it exudes. Inside, the atmosphere is charged, not with the usual hustle of corporate activity, but with an almost palpable sense of ambition.

While most corporations are content with chasing quarterly profits, BlackStone operates on a different plane. Their boardroom discussions aren't just about revenue streams or market shares; they're about controlling those very markets. "Profits are for those who play the game," remarks the enigmatic CEO, Mr. Lysander, during a high-level meeting, "We're here to design the game itself."

Across the vast mahogany table, executives nod in agreement. Each one was handpicked not just for their business acumen but for their shared vision of a world under BlackStone's thumb. Helena, the Chief Strategy Officer, leans forward, her eyes gleaming with a mix of ambition and cunning. "Our assets already rival the GDP of many nations. But it's not just about the wealth; it's about wielding it to shape global events, economies, even governments."

A hush falls over the room as Mr. Lysander stands, gazing out of the floor-to-ceiling windows, looking over the city that never sleeps. "Every heartbeat of this global economy," he muses, "should resonate with our influence. Every decision made, every policy drafted, every currency traded should bear our imprint."

A junior executive, new to the inner circle and eager to make his mark, ventures a question, "But sir, what's the endgame? Is it just about the money?"

Mr. Lysander turns, a cold smile playing on his lips. "Money is a tool, young man. Control is the prize. We're not here to be a footnote in the annals of business history. We're here to write those annals."

The message is clear. BlackStone's vast financial empire, with assets that overshadow many nations, isn't just a testament to their business prowess. It's a monument to their relentless pursuit of an overarching vision: a world where every economic pulse, every political move, every societal shift is orchestrated from the shadows of their boardroom, furthering their dark ambition of absolute global dominance.

The Shadow Over Industries

In the heart of Silicon Valley, a clandestine meeting takes place. The setting is an upscale, dimly lit restaurant, where the who's who of the tech world often gather, away from prying eyes. At a secluded corner table, a top executive from Apple nervously fidgets with his glass of vintage wine. Across from him sits a sharply dressed representative from BlackStone, Ms. Valeria, known in hushed tones as the "Shadow Broker" of the corporate world.

"You know, our latest iPhone model is set to revolutionize the market," the Apple executive begins, trying to steer the conversation towards safer waters.

Ms. Valeria merely smiles, her eyes cold and calculating. "That's all well and good, but let's discuss the real reason we're here. The new software integration, I believe BlackStone and GlobeGuard should have a more... significant role in its development."

The executive gulps, realizing the weight of the implication. "But that would mean giving you access to..."

"Everything," she interrupts smoothly. "Every piece of data, every user interaction, every transaction. Think of the possibilities."

Meanwhile, halfway across the world in Atlanta, a similar scene unfolds. The CEO of Coca-Cola receives a sleek, black envelope. Inside, a single card with just one line: "Consider adding Ingredient X to the next batch. - GG." No explanation, no details, just a veiled directive from GlobeGuard.

Back in Silicon Valley, the Apple executive hesitates. "Such a move would be unprecedented. The backlash..."

Ms. Valeria leans in, her voice dripping with menace. "You misunderstand. This isn't a request. It's a directive. And as for backlash, leave that to us. Giants like Microsoft, PepsiCo, even your direct competitors, have already seen the benefits of our... collaboration."

The message is unmistakably clear. Companies, no matter how colossal, find themselves ensnared in the intricate web spun by BlackStone and GlobeGuard. Their reach is vast, their influence undeniable. From the software that powers our devices to the very ingredients in our drinks, the shadow of these financial titans looms large, dictating terms and shaping industries to further their insidious quest for global dominance.

The Dance of Corporate Giants

In the opulent ballroom of a grand European chateau, the world's most influential corporate leaders gather for the annual "Symposium of Titans." The chandelier overhead casts a golden glow, and the air is thick with anticipation. This isn't just any event; it's where deals are struck, alliances are forged, and the future of industries is decided.

As the evening progresses, a hush falls over the crowd. The spotlight turns to the center of the room, where two figures step onto the dance floor: Mr. Lysander, the enigmatic CEO of BlackStone, and Ms. Eleanor

Whitmore, the visionary leader of a tech conglomerate. Their dance is a mesmerizing tango, a display of power and precision.

Whispers fill the room. "Every step they take, every move they make, it's all pre-decided," murmurs a pharmaceutical magnate to his companion, a media mogul. "We might lead our industries, but in this dance, we're all just following BlackStone's lead."

As Kane and Whitmore glide across the floor, their dance tells a story. Each twirl, each dip represents a business deal, a merger, a strategic shift. The audience, comprising industry leaders, watches intently, trying to decipher the hidden messages in their movements.

Suddenly, Kane pulls Whitmore close, whispering something in her ear. She nods subtly, and as they part, a new pair takes the floor. This time, it's representatives from the automotive and energy sectors. Their dance, a passionate flamenco, speaks of new collaborations, of a future where electric vehicles dominate the roads, all under BlackStone's watchful eye.

Throughout the night, the dance continues, with leaders from various sectors showcasing their "partnerships" with BlackStone. But to the discerning eye, it's evident: this isn't just a dance. It's a display of allegiance, a testament to BlackStone's unparalleled influence.

As dawn approaches, the ballroom slowly empties, but the implications of the night's events are clear. In the grand theater of global industries, while corporate giants may take the stage, it's BlackStone that choreographs the performance, ensuring that every move aligns with their dark vision of global dominance.

The Underlying Ambition

In the dimly lit, wood-paneled boardroom of BlackStone's headquarters, a meeting of the inner circle is underway. The room, adorned with priceless artifacts and paintings of past empire builders, exudes an aura of power.

At the head of the long mahogany table sits Mr. Alexander Kane, his fingers steepled, eyes piercing through the dim light.

"Power," he begins, his voice a low rumble, "is not just about wealth. It's about shaping destinies, molding the future to our vision."

A younger executive, eager to prove his worth, chimes in, "Sir, our assets and investments already give us unparalleled influence. Why seek more?"

Kane leans forward, the weight of his ambition evident in his gaze. "Imagine a world where every major decision, every turn of events, is influenced by us. Where nations look to us for direction, where we don't just predict the future; we create it."

A murmur of agreement ripples through the room. Eleanor Whitmore, the astute tech magnate from the dance, speaks up, "It's not just about controlling markets, Alex. It's about crafting narratives, influencing ideologies, ensuring that the world moves to our orchestrated symphony."

Kane nods, appreciating her insight. "Exactly, Eleanor. The true allure lies in being the puppet masters of history. To not just witness but dictate the rise and fall of empires, to shape the stories that future generations will read about."

The room falls silent, each member lost in the grandeur of the vision Kane has painted. The intoxication of such power, the allure of playing god in the theater of global events, is a heady sensation.

As the meeting concludes, it's clear that BlackStone's ambitions are not just about financial dominance. Their goal is to etch their name into the annals of history, to be the unseen hand that guides the fate of nations. And in this relentless pursuit, ethics, morality, and the greater good are but mere obstacles to be maneuvered around.

A Calculated Game of Chess

The sun was setting, casting a golden hue over the sprawling BlackStone estate. Inside, a grand room was illuminated by a massive crystal chandelier. In the center stood a colossal chessboard, each piece meticulously carved from precious stones. The kings stood tall, representing the might of nations, while the pawns, though smaller, were no less significant, symbolizing the countless corporations under BlackStone's influence.

Sebastian Gray, BlackStone's Chief Strategist, stood on one side of the board, his sharp eyes analyzing every piece. Opposite him was Lucinda Vale, the company's top analyst, known for her uncanny ability to predict global market shifts.

"This move," Sebastian said, pointing to a knight, which represented a recent acquisition in the tech sector, "gives us control over the digital data streams of three continents."

Lucinda smirked, moving her bishop forward, symbolizing BlackStone's influence in the European energy market. "And with this, we can manipulate energy prices, causing ripples in their economies, making them more pliable to our demands."

Sebastian chuckled, appreciating the audacity of the move. "It's all interconnected, Lucinda. Like a game of chess, every move we make, no matter how insignificant it may seem, has consequences. Consequences that further our grip on the global stage."

Lucinda leaned in, her voice dropping to a whisper, "And what's the endgame, Sebastian? Checkmate?"

He paused, letting the weight of the question hang in the air. "Complete and utter dominance. A world where BlackStone doesn't just participate in global events but dictates them. Where nations, leaders, and economies bend to our will."

The two continued their game, each move echoing the real-world maneuvers of BlackStone. As the night deepened, it became evident that this wasn't just a casual game between colleagues. It was a representation of BlackStone's global strategy, a calculated dance of power and influence, where the endgame was nothing less than world dominance.

Unraveling the Grand Vision

In the heart of New York City, within the towering skyscrapers that touch the heavens, lies the BlackStone headquarters. A monolithic structure of glass and steel, it stands as a testament to the company's might and influence. Inside, the atmosphere is electric, buzzing with the energy of a thousand minds working in unison, all dedicated to realizing BlackStone's grand vision.

In a dimly lit conference room, a massive screen displays a digital web, each node representing a facet of BlackStone's vast empire. Helena Wraith, BlackStone's enigmatic CSO, stands before it, her fingers tracing the various connections, her eyes reflecting the ambition that has driven the company to its current heights.

"Every thread you see here," she begins, addressing a select group of top-tier executives, "represents years of planning, of maneuvering, of strategic positioning. We're not just building a company; we're crafting a legacy."

Marcus Flint, the head of BlackStone's European operations, leans forward, intrigued. "And what is the end goal, Helena? What does this legacy look like?"

Helena smirks, her gaze unwavering. "A world where BlackStone isn't just a name, but a force. A force that dictates global trends, shapes economies, and influences the destinies of nations."

A murmur of approval ripples through the room. Victoria Lane, a recent addition to the BlackStone team but a veteran in global finance, raises an eyebrow. "It's an audacious vision, Helena. But how do we ensure that we remain unchallenged, that no other entity can rival our dominance?"

Helena's smile widens, revealing a hint of the ruthlessness that has made her a legend in the corporate world. "By staying ahead, always. By predicting the future, molding it to our design, and ensuring that every move, every decision, is a step towards our ultimate goal."

As the meeting progresses, it becomes evident that BlackStone's vision isn't just about financial dominance. It's about rewriting the rules of the game, about ensuring that the world dances to their tune. It's a tale of unparalleled ambition, of a company that doesn't just want to play the game but wants to own it. And as we delve deeper into their strategies, their alliances, and their machinations, we begin to understand the true depth of their desire to stand unrivaled on the global stage.

Chapter 2
The Aladdin Network

The Silent Operator in Global Finance

Deep within the bowels of BlackStone's state-of-the-art headquarters, a room hums with the ceaseless activity of servers and supercomputers. This is the heart of Aladdin, a technological behemoth that stands as a testament to BlackStone's audacious ambitions. Encased in layers of security, both digital and physical, Aladdin is more than just a system; it's the embodiment of BlackStone's desire to control the world's financial pulse.

As the sun sets, casting long shadows across the city, a select group gathers in a secure conference room overlooking the sprawling metropolis. The room's centerpiece is a massive holographic display, showcasing real-time data streams from global markets, all being processed and analyzed by Aladdin.

"Aladdin isn't just a tool," begins Dr. Adrian Vale, the chief architect behind the system, his voice filled with a mix of pride and reverence. "It's an entity, a silent observer that sees all, knows all, and most importantly, predicts all."

Lena Rostov, a senior executive at BlackStone, leans in, her eyes reflecting the city lights. "So, Adrian, in layman's terms, Aladdin gives us the ability to...?"

"To control the narrative," Dr. Vale interrupts, a sly smile playing on his lips. "With Aladdin, we're not just reacting to market shifts; we're orchestrating them. It anticipates global economic movements, allowing BlackStone to be not just one, but several steps ahead."

A murmur of appreciation fills the room. Victor Grimes, a seasoned investor known for his skepticism, raises an eyebrow. "Impressive, but how do we ensure that Aladdin remains our secret weapon? That it doesn't fall into the wrong hands?"

Dr. Vale chuckles, "Aladdin is designed to be impenetrable. Its core algorithms are encrypted in ways that even I can't decipher without the right keys. And those keys," he pauses, glancing at a secure vault embedded in the room's wall, "are safeguarded with utmost care."

As the night deepens, the group delves further into the capabilities of Aladdin, discussing strategies, potential scenarios, and the vast opportunities that lie ahead. It becomes clear that with Aladdin, BlackStone isn't just playing the game of global finance; they're rewriting its rules. And in this high-stakes game, Aladdin is their silent ace, ensuring that their dark ambitions for global dominance remain unchallenged.

More Than Just Data Analysis

In a sleek, dimly lit room adorned with multiple screens, a team of BlackStone's brightest data scientists and analysts huddle around a central console. The air is thick with anticipation. The screens display a flurry of numbers, graphs, and codes, all flowing seamlessly, all being processed by Aladdin.

"Most systems," began Dr. Helena Carter, BlackStone's lead data strategist, her voice echoing in the hushed room, "are designed to merely react to the present. They analyze, they interpret, and they report. But Aladdin," she paused, a glint of mischief in her eyes, "Aladdin foresees."

A junior analyst, Mark, couldn't contain his curiosity. "So, you're saying Aladdin can predict future market movements?"

Dr. Carter nodded, "Exactly, Mark. But it goes beyond mere prediction. Aladdin can manipulate variables, test scenarios, and even orchestrate certain market outcomes. It's like playing a game of chess where you can see not just your opponent's next move, but their next ten."

Ricardo Silva, BlackStone's VP of Operations, leaned forward, intrigued. "Give us a demonstration, Helena."

Dr. Carter gestured to the main screen. "Let's take the European bond market, for instance. If we input certain variables..." She quickly typed in a series of commands, and the screen came alive with simulations. "Aladdin can show us potential outcomes based on current trends, geopolitical events, even social media sentiment. And then," she smirked, "it can suggest interventions to sway the market in our favor."

The room watched in awe as Aladdin played out multiple scenarios, each ending with BlackStone gaining a strategic advantage. It was a masterclass in manipulation, a showcase of power that only BlackStone wielded.

Silva let out a low whistle. "This isn't just being ahead of the game. This is rewriting the rulebook."

Dr. Carter smiled, her gaze fixed on the screens. "With Aladdin, BlackStone doesn't play by the market's rules. The market plays by BlackStone's."

As the team delved deeper into Aladdin's capabilities, it became evident that this wasn't just a tool; it was a weapon. A weapon that BlackStone would wield with precision and ruthlessness in their relentless quest for global dominance.

The Enigmatic Algorithms

In a secure, soundproof chamber deep within BlackStone's headquarters, a select group of the world's top mathematicians and coders convene. This is the heart of Aladdin, where its most guarded secrets reside. The room is cold, both in temperature and ambiance, with walls lined with servers that hum with raw computational power.

Dr. Aiden Fletcher, the chief architect behind Aladdin's algorithms, stands at a holographic interface, fingers dancing over the projections. "Most algorithms," he began, his voice echoing with a mix of pride and caution, "are reactive. They're designed based on past data, past trends. But Aladdin's algorithms," he paused, letting the weight of his words sink in, "they're predictive. They don't just learn; they anticipate."

A young coder, Li Na, raised her hand hesitantly. "Dr. Fletcher, I've heard rumors that Aladdin can predict global economic shifts. Is that true?"

Fletcher smiled enigmatically. "Rumors have a grain of truth, Li Na. But it's more than just prediction. Aladdin's algorithms analyze patterns, geopolitical events, even seemingly unrelated global incidents, and weave them into a tapestry of potential futures."

Another member, Professor Ivanov, a renowned economist, chimed in, "So, you're suggesting that while we're analyzing quarterly reports, Aladdin is looking at political elections, natural disasters, technological breakthroughs, and even cultural shifts?"

"Exactly," Fletcher affirmed. "It sees the butterfly effect in real-time. A minor policy change in a small European country, a technological breakthrough in Silicon Valley, a cultural revolution in Africa – Aladdin processes these and predicts their ripple effects on the global economy."

The room was silent, the magnitude of Aladdin's capabilities dawning on everyone present.

Li Na, her eyes wide with a mix of awe and fear, whispered, "It's like... it's like Aladdin has a crystal ball."

Fletcher nodded, his gaze distant. "Yes, but with this power comes immense responsibility. And in the hands of BlackStone," he sighed, "it's a tool to shape the world as they see fit."

As the meeting continued, the group delved deeper into the intricacies of Aladdin's algorithms. But one thing was clear: BlackStone, with Aladdin's foresight, was playing a game where they held all the cards, and the world was none the wiser.

The Exclusive "Aladdin Climate" App

In the opulent penthouse suite of a towering skyscraper, a gathering of the world's wealthiest individuals convened. The room was filled with the soft hum of conversations, the clinking of glasses, and an underlying current of anticipation. At the center of this gathering stood a sleek, holographic display showcasing the logo of the "Aladdin Climate" app.

A hush fell over the room as Damien Blackwood, BlackStone's charismatic VP of Technological Innovations, took the stage. "Ladies and gentlemen," he began, his voice dripping with charm, "tonight, I present to you not just an app, but the future."

With a flourish, he activated the holographic interface, revealing a real-time global map intricately detailed with climate data, investment opportunities, and predictive economic shifts. "The 'Aladdin Climate' app," Damien continued, "is our crown jewel. While the world sees climate change as a challenge, we see it as an opportunity."

Lord Harrington, an oil magnate, leaned over to whisper to his companion, tech billionaire Elara Sinclair, "This isn't just about tracking carbon footprints, is it?"

Elara, her eyes fixed on the display, replied, "No, it's about predicting where the next goldmine is. Whether it's a drought-stricken region ripe for a water supply project or an area projected to become the next tech hub due to climate migrations, this app tells you where to invest."

Damien, sensing the growing interest, delved deeper. "Imagine knowing which coastal cities will face the most significant challenges in the next decade and where to invest in real estate inland. Or predicting which crops will fail and where to funnel your agricultural investments."

A murmur of appreciation rippled through the room.

Madame Lefevre, a French vineyard heiress, raised her champagne flute and remarked, "So, while the world scrambles to adapt, we're always ten steps ahead, capitalizing on every shift. C'est magnifique!"

Damien nodded, a sly smile playing on his lips. "Exactly, Madame Lefevre. While others see chaos, we see a chessboard. And with the 'Aladdin Climate' app, we always know the next move."

As the presentation concluded, it was evident that BlackStone had once again outdone themselves. The "Aladdin Climate" app wasn't just a tool; it was a weapon, ensuring that the world's elite remained not just wealthy but also powerful, all under the watchful eyes of BlackStone's grand vision.

A Facade of Sustainability

In a lavish conference room adorned with gold leaf and mahogany, a select group of influential figures gathered around a long, polished table. The room's ambiance was thick with tension, the kind that precedes significant revelations. At the head of the table, a large screen displayed the "Aladdin Climate" app's interface, its green logo gleaming promisingly.

Aria Sterling, a renowned environmental activist, and journalist, was the first to break the silence. "I've been hearing a lot about this app," she began, her voice laced with skepticism. "It's being hailed as the beacon of sustainability, the solution to our climate woes. But I've also heard whispers that there's more to it than meets the eye."

Sebastian Kane, BlackStone's Chief Strategy Officer, leaned back in his chair, a smirk playing on his lips. "Ms. Sterling, every tool has its purpose. The 'Aladdin Climate' app is designed to identify green investment opportunities. But, of course, in the world of finance, every opportunity also presents... advantages."

Lord Harrington, the oil magnate from the previous gathering, chuckled. "Advantages? Is that what we're calling them now? Let's cut to the chase.

This app tells us where the next disaster will strike, where the next flood, drought, or wildfire will be. And with that knowledge, we can buy up land, resources, and even governments at a fraction of the price."

Aria's eyes widened in realization. "So, while the world sees BlackStone as the champion of sustainability, you're actually profiting from the very disasters that climate change brings?"

Sebastian raised an eyebrow, his smirk deepening. "It's all a matter of perspective, Ms. Sterling. While others see calamities, we see... opportunities."

Madame Lefevre, sipping her wine, added, "And with every crisis, our influence grows. We're not just investing in the future; we're shaping it."

Aria, her voice trembling with anger, retorted, "You're playing with the lives of millions, all for your insatiable greed!"

Sebastian leaned forward, his gaze cold and calculating. "In this world, Ms. Sterling, there are those who watch things happen, those who wonder what happened, and those who make things happen. At BlackStone, we've always been the latter."

As the meeting adjourned, it was clear that the "Aladdin Climate" app was more than just a technological marvel. It was a testament to BlackStone's cunning, their ability to wear the mask of sustainability while exploiting the very crises they claimed to combat.

Profiteering from Global Challenges

The sun was setting over the sprawling city, casting a golden hue over the BlackStone headquarters. Inside, a group of the world's most influential power players gathered in a dimly lit room, the walls of which were adorned with screens displaying real-time data from various parts of the globe. Each screen showed a different scene: wildfires raging, floods inundating cities, droughts parching lands. But instead of concern, the room was filled with an air of anticipation.

Dmitri Volkov, a Russian oligarch with vast interests in the oil industry, took a sip from his glass and remarked, "It's fascinating, isn't it? While the world sees these as calamities, we see them as... opportunities."

Liliana Mendoza, a tech mogul from South America, nodded in agreement. "Every crisis is a business opportunity in disguise. And with Aladdin's predictive capabilities, we're always one step ahead."

A hush fell over the room as the CEO of BlackStone stepped forward. "Ladies and gentlemen," he began, his voice dripping with authority, "the world is changing. And while others see challenges, we see potential. Potential to reshape industries, control resources, and dictate the future."

He gestured to a screen displaying a drought-stricken region. "Take this, for instance. As water becomes scarce, its value increases. With Aladdin's insights, we've already secured rights to major water sources in the area. When the time comes, we won't just be selling water; we'll be selling life."

A murmur of approval rippled through the room.

Rajiv Mehta, a real estate tycoon from India, chimed in, "And as sea levels rise, coastal properties will be underwater, both literally and financially. Thanks to Aladdin, I've shifted my investments to higher grounds, ensuring maximum returns."

Lysander smiled, "Exactly. While the world scrambles to adapt, we're already positioned to profit. Every challenge, every crisis, is a chance for us to expand our empire."

A young journalist, who had managed to infiltrate the meeting, felt a chill run down her spine. She had heard rumors of BlackStone's ambitions, but the sheer audacity of their plans was staggering. As she discreetly recorded the conversation, she realized that this wasn't just about profiteering. It was about control, dominance, and reshaping the world in BlackStone's image.

The Ultimate Goal: Control

The opulent boardroom of BlackStone was abuzz with activity. Massive screens displayed real-time data, stock market trends, and global news. At the head of the long mahogany table sat Helena Blackwood, her fingers steepled, eyes scanning the room filled with her trusted lieutenants.

"Aladdin has given us a glimpse into the future," she began, her voice cold and calculated. "A future where we don't just participate; we dictate."

A holo-projection in the center of the table illuminated a 3D model of the Earth, with various regions highlighted. "These," she pointed, "are the world's most crucial resource points. Water reservoirs in Africa, mineral mines in South America, energy hubs in Asia. Control these, and you control the world."

Xavier, BlackStone's chief strategist, stepped forward, adjusting his glasses. "With Aladdin's predictive capabilities, we've identified potential flashpoints and opportunities. Political instabilities, economic downturns, even natural disasters. Where others see chaos, we see a chance to consolidate our grip."

Helena's lips curled into a smile, "Exactly. As nations grapple with these challenges, they'll turn to us. Not just for resources, but for direction. And we'll be ready."

A murmur of agreement spread across the room.

Lucia, a top executive with ties to European governments, added, "I've already initiated talks with several leaders. They're desperate, Helena. With the right push, they'll dance to our tune."

Helena leaned back, her gaze fixed on the rotating Earth projection. "This is just the beginning. As the world stands on the brink of unprecedented change, we won't just be observers. We'll be the puppeteers."

A silence enveloped the room, each member absorbing the gravity of their mission. It wasn't just about wealth or influence. It was about legacy, about etching BlackStone's name into the annals of history as the entity that reshaped the world.

A young intern, who had been silent throughout the meeting, finally mustered the courage to speak. "But at what cost? What about the people, the societies we'll disrupt?"

Helena turned her icy gaze to him. "Progress always comes at a price. And we're willing to pay it. The question is, are you?"

The intern swallowed hard, realizing the depth of BlackStone's ambition. This wasn't just business; it was a quest for global dominance, with Aladdin as their compass.

Chapter 3
The Green Mirage

The Environmental Champion?

The grand ballroom of the Ritz-Carlton was adorned with banners proclaiming BlackStone's commitment to a greener future. The room buzzed with anticipation as journalists, environmentalists, and business magnates gathered for BlackStone's annual "Green Future Summit."

At the center of the stage stood a massive ice sculpture of the Earth, slowly melting under the spotlight, symbolizing the urgency of the climate crisis. As the attendees took their seats, a hush fell over the room, and the lights dimmed.

From the shadows emerged Helena Blackwood, BlackStone's charismatic CSO. Dressed in a green silk gown, she approached the podium, her eyes scanning the audience. "Good evening, esteemed guests. Tonight, we stand at the crossroads of history. The climate crisis is real, and BlackStone is committed to leading the charge towards a sustainable future."

The audience erupted in applause, captivated by Helena's words. But in a corner of the room, investigative journalist Lara Mitchell wasn't so easily swayed. She had been tracking BlackStone's activities for years and had her suspicions.

As Helena unveiled a series of green initiatives, from renewable energy projects to sustainable agriculture investments, Lara whispered to her colleague, "It all sounds too good to be true. Since when did BlackStone care about the environment?"

Her colleague, Mark, a seasoned environmental reporter, replied, "It's all a facade, Lara. They're using the climate crisis as a smokescreen to further their global ambitions. While the world lauds their green initiatives, they're quietly consolidating power behind the scenes."

Lara jotted down notes, her mind racing. "We need to dig deeper, Mark. There's more to this 'Green Mirage' than meets the eye."

As the summit continued, Helena announced a partnership with a renowned environmental NGO, further solidifying BlackStone's image as a champion of sustainability. But as the applause echoed through the ballroom, those in the know couldn't help but wonder: Was BlackStone truly the environmental savior they claimed to be, or was this just another chapter in their quest for global dominance?

CEO Larry Lysander's Climate Rhetoric

The sun was setting over Manhattan, casting a golden hue over the city's iconic skyline. Inside the luxurious penthouse suite of the BlackStone Tower, a select group of Wall Street's elite gathered for an exclusive dinner hosted by none other than Larry Lysander, the enigmatic CEO of BlackStone.

As the guests mingled, sipping on vintage champagne and discussing the latest market trends, a large screen displayed images of melting glaciers, forest fires, and devastating hurricanes. The message was clear: the planet was in peril.

Taking his position at the head of the long mahogany table, Larry raised his glass for a toast. "To a sustainable future," he declared, his voice filled with conviction. The room echoed in agreement, glasses clinking in unison.

As the evening progressed, Larry, with his characteristic charisma, delved into the heart of the matter. "Climate change isn't just an environmental issue; it's a financial one," he began. "The risks it poses to our investments are real and imminent. We, at BlackStone, recognize these challenges and are committed to steering our investments towards a greener future."

Across the table, Sophia Turner, a renowned environmental journalist, exchanged a skeptical glance with her colleague. She had heard these speeches before, and while Larry's words were compelling, she couldn't help but question their authenticity.

During the Q&A session, she seized the opportunity. "Mr. Fink," she began, her voice steady, "While your commitment to addressing climate risks is commendable, how do you reconcile this with BlackStone's investments in industries known for their environmental impact?"

Larry, ever the seasoned speaker, responded with a well-rehearsed answer about balancing profits with responsibility. But Sophia wasn't convinced. She leaned over to her colleague and whispered, "There's more to this than meets the eye. Larry's climate rhetoric is too polished, too perfect. It's all part of a bigger game."

As the evening drew to a close, Larry's words about sustainability and responsibility continued to resonate with many of the attendees. But for those who dared to look beyond the surface, the question remained: Was BlackStone's CEO genuinely concerned about the planet, or was his climate rhetoric just another piece in their strategic game of global dominance?

The Climate Change Narrative

The bustling city of Davos was abuzz with anticipation. The World Economic Forum was in full swing, and leaders from across the globe had descended upon the picturesque Swiss town. Among the myriad of topics on the agenda, climate change was the most hotly debated. And at the center of this discourse was BlackStone.

In a grand hall adorned with crystal chandeliers and opulent drapes, a panel discussion titled "The Future of Our Planet" was underway. The audience, a mix of world leaders, CEOs, activists, and journalists, hung on to every word. Among the panelists was Dr. Helena Martinez, a renowned climate scientist, and next to her sat Richard Grayson, BlackStone's Chief Sustainability Officer.

"As we all know," began Dr. Martinez, her voice filled with urgency, "our planet is at a tipping point. The science is clear, and the time for action is now." She presented a series of graphs and data, painting a grim picture of the world's climate trajectory.

Richard, adjusting his tie, took the microphone. "At BlackStone," he began with a confident tone, "we recognize the gravity of the situation. That's why we're committed to leading the charge in sustainable investments." He went on to detail BlackStone's green initiatives, emphasizing their dedication to the cause.

In the audience, investigative journalist Alex Rourke scribbled notes. He had been tracking BlackStone's activities for years and had always been skeptical of their environmental claims. Turning to his colleague, he whispered, "It's all too convenient, isn't it? BlackStone suddenly championing the climate cause just as it becomes a global focus."

His colleague, Lara, nodded in agreement. "It's classic BlackStone. They see an opportunity in every crisis. While the world is genuinely concerned about the environment, they're looking for ways to capitalize on it."

Later that evening, at a private reception, Alex approached Richard. "Mr. Grayson," he began, offering a firm handshake, "Your talk today was impressive. But I'm curious, how does BlackStone reconcile its green initiatives with its investments in fossil fuels?"

Richard, taken aback by the directness of the question, took a moment before replying, "We believe in a balanced approach, Alex. Transitioning to a green economy takes time, and we're doing our part."

But Alex wasn't convinced. As he walked away, he couldn't help but wonder: Was BlackStone's involvement in the climate change narrative genuine, or was it just another strategic move in their quest for global dominance?

The ESG Movement and BlackStone's Role

The sun was setting over Manhattan, casting a golden hue over the city's iconic skyline. Inside a plush penthouse suite, a group of influential individuals gathered for an exclusive event. The occasion? The launch of a new ESG fund by BlackStone.

Amidst the clinking of champagne glasses and soft jazz playing in the background, Sarah Mitchell, a prominent environmental activist, found herself in a heated discussion with Mark Harrison, BlackStone's Head of ESG Initiatives.

"You know, Mark," Sarah began, her voice dripping with skepticism, "the ESG movement began as a grassroots effort. It was about genuine change, about making corporations accountable. But with giants like BlackStone jumping on the bandwagon, I fear the essence is getting lost."

Mark, ever the smooth operator, replied with a practiced ease, "Sarah, I understand your concerns. But think about the scale and impact a company like BlackStone can bring. We have the resources and the reach to make a real difference."

Sarah raised an eyebrow. "Or to hijack the movement for your own gains?" she retorted. "I've seen reports of BlackStone's investments in industries that are anything but sustainable. How do you reconcile that with your so-called commitment to ESG?"

Mark took a sip of his drink, choosing his words carefully. "It's a transition, Sarah. We can't change overnight. But our involvement in ESG is a step in the right direction."

Across the room, journalist Maya Jensen overheard their conversation. She had been researching the corporatization of the ESG movement and had her reservations about BlackStone's role. Approaching a colleague, she whispered, "It's all a bit convenient, isn't it? BlackStone suddenly championing ESG just as it becomes a hot topic. Makes you wonder if they're genuinely committed or if they're just trying to control the narrative."

Her colleague, Roberto, nodded in agreement. "It's a classic power play. They see a movement gaining traction, and they want in. Not necessarily for the right reasons, but to ensure they're in a position to steer it."

As the evening wore on, the discussions around BlackStone's involvement in the ESG movement continued. While some saw their participation as a positive step, others couldn't shake off the feeling that it was just another strategy in BlackStone's playbook, intertwining political and social motives to further their global dominance.

A Smokescreen for True Intentions

The rain pattered softly against the windows of a dimly lit room in downtown London. Inside, a group of environmentalists, journalists, and analysts gathered for a covert meeting. The topic? BlackStone's sudden and fervent support for ESG.

Emma Thompson, a renowned environmentalist, took the floor. "Ladies and gentlemen," she began, her voice echoing with conviction, "we've seen corporations pay lip service to environmental causes before. But BlackStone's recent foray into ESG is on an entirely different scale. Their campaigns, their investments, their PR stunts... it all seems too orchestrated."

A journalist named Alex chimed in, "I attended their last ESG conference. The production value, the celebrity endorsements, the grand promises... it felt more like a Hollywood production than an earnest commitment to the environment."

Emma nodded, "Exactly. It's all a show, a smokescreen. While the world is dazzled by their 'green initiatives,' what's happening behind the scenes?"

A young analyst, Ravi, shuffled some papers in front of him. "I've been tracking their investments. For every green project they fund, there are several others that raise eyebrows. Mining projects, oil ventures, industries notorious for their carbon footprint. It's as if they're playing both sides."

A murmur of agreement swept the room.

Lucia, a seasoned environmental lawyer, added, "It's a classic diversion tactic. By loudly championing ESG, they divert attention from their more controversial endeavors. And under this guise of environmental concern, they're strategically positioning themselves in sectors that will give them even more control on the global stage."

Emma leaned forward, her eyes scanning the room. "We need to expose this. The world deserves to know that BlackStone's 'environmental concern' might just be a facade to further their global ambitions."

Alex, tapping his pen thoughtfully, replied, "It won't be easy. They have resources, connections, and a narrative that the world wants to believe. But we have the truth."

As the rain outside intensified, so did the resolve of the individuals in the room. They knew they were up against a giant, but they were determined to unveil the reality behind BlackStone's smokescreen.

Controlling the Climate Narrative

The sun was setting over Geneva, casting a golden hue over the city's iconic Jet d'Eau. Inside a plush conference room overlooking Lake Geneva, a group of influential policymakers, environmentalists, and business leaders gathered for the annual Global Climate Summit. The event was sponsored by none other than BlackStone.

As attendees mingled, sipping on sustainably sourced wines and discussing the latest in green technology, a large screen at the front of the room played a montage of BlackStone's environmental initiatives. Solar farms, wind turbines, reforestation projects – it was an impressive display of commitment to the planet.

However, in a quiet corner of the room, Dr. Helena Martinez, a climate scientist, and Rajiv Mehta, an investigative journalist, exchanged skeptical glances.

"Have you noticed," Rajiv whispered, "how BlackStone's narrative conveniently aligns with the most popular and media-friendly aspects of sustainability? It's as if they're cherry-picking the parts of the climate conversation that best serve their interests."

Helena nodded, "Exactly. While it's commendable that they're investing in renewable energy, there's little mention of their involvement in sectors that are less 'green'. It's a selective narrative, and it's steering the global conversation in a direction that benefits them."

Rajiv took a sip of his drink, "And it's not just about the investments. Have you seen the policy proposals they've been backing? They're pushing for regulations that would give them tax breaks, subsidies, and even exclusive rights to certain green technologies."

Helena raised an eyebrow, "So, under the guise of environmental concern, they're essentially setting themselves up to monopolize the very solutions the world is turning to. It's genius, in a diabolical sort of way."

Rajiv leaned in closer, "I've been digging into their ties with global policymakers. It's astonishing how many of them have BlackStone connections, either through campaign donations, personal relationships, or business ventures."

Helena sighed, "The world is desperate for climate solutions, and BlackStone is offering them on a silver platter. But at what cost? They're not just influencing the narrative; they're controlling it."

As the evening wore on, the duo realized the enormity of the challenge ahead. BlackStone's "Green Mirage" was not just a PR campaign; it was a meticulously crafted strategy to reshape the global response to climate change, ensuring they remained at the helm of power.

Unmasking the Green Façade

The sun had barely risen over the bustling city of New York, but inside a discreet penthouse suite, a clandestine meeting was already in full swing. The room, adorned with minimalist decor and panoramic views of the skyline, was filled with a palpable tension. At the head of the sleek mahogany table sat Victor Kane, BlackStone's Chief Strategy Officer, flanked by a team of the company's top environmental consultants and PR experts.

"Alright, let's get straight to it," Victor began, his voice dripping with authority. "Our green initiatives have been receiving a lot of attention lately, and while the public adoration is good for our image, we need to ensure that our underlying objectives remain concealed."

A young consultant, Clara, cleared her throat, "The reforestation project in Brazil has garnered positive press. It's been a fantastic distraction from our mining interests in the region."

Victor smirked, "Exactly. Plant a few trees, and no one notices the mountains we're leveling in the background. But we need more. The world is watching, and we need to be seen as the champions of sustainability."

An older gentleman, Dr. Geoffrey Hartman, a renowned environmental scientist now on BlackStone's payroll, chimed in, "We could fund research into sustainable agriculture. It would give us control over food supply chains and divert attention from our less environmentally-friendly ventures."

Victor nodded, "Good. What else?"

A PR expert, Lila, suggested, "How about a global campaign promoting clean energy? We could host summits, workshops, and even partner with celebrities. It would solidify our image as leaders in the fight against climate change."

Victor leaned back, absorbing the suggestions. "All good ideas. But remember, every move we make, every initiative we launch, has to serve our ultimate goal: global dominance. We're not in this for the planet; we're in it for power."

As the meeting continued, the depth of BlackStone's manipulation became clear. Beneath the veneer of their green initiatives lay a web of strategies designed to further their global ambitions. They weren't just playing the game; they were rewriting the rules.

This chapter, through a series of revelations, interviews, and investigative reports, aims to pull back the curtain on BlackStone's green façade. As we delve deeper into their environmental posturing, the line between genuine concern and corporate greed becomes alarmingly thin. The world may see them as saviors, but beneath the surface, their intentions are far from noble. Their green initiatives, while commendable on the surface, are but pieces in a much larger, more sinister puzzle: a master plan to control and dominate the global stage.

Chapter 4
The Woke Ideology: A Mask for Manipulation

The Rise of 'Woke' and BlackStone's Embrace

The bustling streets of San Francisco, known for its tech giants and progressive culture, were alive with the chants of thousands. "Justice now!" they cried, their voices echoing off the city's iconic buildings. Among the sea of protesters, banners with slogans advocating for various social causes waved in the wind. The 'woke' movement, once a fringe idea, had now become mainstream, capturing the hearts and minds of millions worldwide.

In a sleek, high-rise office overlooking the protest, two figures watched the scene below. One was Diana Mitchell, BlackStone's Chief Marketing Officer, and the other, a renowned sociologist, Dr. Marcus Green.

"It's fascinating," Dr. Green mused, adjusting his glasses. "The 'woke' movement has transformed from a grassroots campaign into a global phenomenon in just a few years."

Diana nodded, her sharp eyes assessing the crowd. "It's more than just a movement, Marcus. It's a powerful narrative, and narratives shape perceptions. If BlackStone can align with this, we can shape those perceptions to our advantage."

Dr. Green raised an eyebrow, intrigued. "So, you're suggesting BlackStone should adopt the 'woke' ideology?"

Diana smirked, "Not just adopt, Marcus. We need to champion it. Imagine the possibilities. By positioning ourselves at the forefront of social justice, we can divert attention from our more... controversial ventures."

Dr. Green leaned back, processing the implications. "It's a bold move. But it could work. The world is hungry for corporate entities that seem to care. If BlackStone can tap into that sentiment, you'd be unstoppable."

Diana's lips curled into a sly smile. "Exactly. It's not about genuine alignment. It's strategy. We don't just want to ride the 'woke' wave; we want to control its direction."

As the conversation continued, it became evident that BlackStone's interest in the 'woke' movement was far from altruistic. While the world saw a company evolving with the times, behind closed doors, it was all a calculated play. BlackStone's embrace of the 'woke' ideology wasn't about social justice or progressive values. It was about power, manipulation, and furthering their dark ambitions in the guise of social responsibility.

A Progressive Facade or Calculated Move?

The sun was setting over New York City, casting a golden hue over the skyline. Inside a luxurious penthouse, a select group of influential figures gathered for an exclusive event hosted by BlackStone. Among the attendees was renowned journalist, Clara Thompson, known for her incisive articles and fearless pursuit of truth.

As she sipped her champagne, Clara's eyes scanned the room, taking in the opulence. The walls were adorned with artwork from renowned artists, and a string quartet played softly in the background. Everywhere she looked, there were discussions about social justice, gender equality, and environmental sustainability. BlackStone seemed to be making all the right noises, aligning themselves with the 'woke' movement.

Approaching Clara was Adrian Foster, BlackStone's Head of Public Relations. "Ms. Thompson," he greeted with a charming smile, "I'm delighted you could join us. I've been an admirer of your work for years."

Clara raised an eyebrow, intrigued. "Thank you, Mr. Foster. I must admit, I'm curious about BlackStone's sudden interest in 'woke' causes. It's quite the departure from your usual business-centric events."

Adrian chuckled, "Times are changing, Ms. Thompson. BlackStone recognizes the importance of social justice and wants to be at the forefront of this change."

Clara took a thoughtful sip of her drink. "It's commendable, but you must understand my skepticism. BlackStone has always been about profits. This sudden shift seems... convenient."

Adrian leaned in, his voice dropping to a conspiratorial whisper. "Between you and me, it's not just about being on the right side of history. It's also about staying relevant, influential, and in control."

Clara's eyes narrowed, sensing a story. "So, it's a strategic move?"

Adrian hesitated for a moment, then sighed. "Every corporation has its strategies, Ms. Thompson. But that doesn't mean our commitment to these causes isn't genuine."

The evening continued, but Clara's mind was racing. BlackStone's support for 'woke' causes might have appeared progressive, but beneath the surface, there seemed to be layers of manipulation and strategy. The challenge now was to discern the genuine intentions from the calculated moves, to uncover the truth behind the facade.

Manipulating Public Sentiment

The bustling streets of Manhattan were alive with protestors. Signs reading "Equality for All" and "Justice Now" were held high, and passionate chants filled the air. Among the sea of protestors was a young activist, Maya, who had dedicated her life to social justice causes.

As Maya led a group in a chant, she noticed a massive digital billboard displaying BlackStone's logo alongside a message: "Standing with you for a just world." The sight gave her pause. She remembered reading about BlackStone's recent alignment with 'woke' causes and their vocal support for social justice. But something felt off.

Later that evening, at a local café, Maya met with her mentor, an older activist named Elijah. Over steaming cups of coffee, she voiced her concerns. "Elijah, why would a financial giant like BlackStone suddenly champion our causes? It doesn't add up."

Elijah leaned back, his eyes thoughtful. "Maya, in the world of global finance and politics, everything is a chess game. Companies like BlackStone don't just make moves; they strategize."

Maya frowned, "So you're saying their support for social justice is just a strategy?"

Elijah nodded, "It's about manipulating public sentiment. Think about it. By aligning with popular social movements, they can influence public opinion, which in turn can sway corporate decisions and political outcomes. It's a way to further their reach and power."

Maya's eyes widened in realization. "So, while we're out here fighting for genuine change, they're using our movement to further their global ambitions?"

Elijah sighed, "It's a possibility. The challenge is to ensure that our movement remains pure and isn't co-opted by corporate interests."

The conversation left Maya with more questions than answers. She realized that the battle for social justice was not just against visible adversaries but also against shadowy entities that sought to manipulate the narrative for their gain. Determined, she knew she had to be vigilant and ensure that the true essence of the movement wasn't diluted by BlackStone's strategic games.

The Power Play Behind 'Woke' Advocacy

In a lavish penthouse overlooking the city, a group of BlackStone's top executives gathered around a polished mahogany table. The room was dimly lit, with the city's lights providing a muted backdrop. At the head of the table sat Victor, BlackStone's Chief Strategy Officer, a man known for his cunning and ability to read the global pulse.

"Public sentiment is shifting," Victor began, his voice smooth and calculated. "The 'woke' movement is gaining momentum, and we need to be at the forefront of this change."

A younger executive, Clara, raised an eyebrow. "Why? We're a financial institution. Why involve ourselves in social justice causes?"

Victor smirked, "Because, my dear, it's all about control. By endorsing these movements, we can steer public opinion. If we can control the narrative, we can influence decisions on a global scale."

Another executive, Raymond, leaned forward, intrigued. "So, we're not genuinely supporting these causes?"

Victor chuckled, "Genuine support is a luxury we can't afford. But if we can appear as champions of these causes, we can manipulate the masses, making them believe we're on their side. This will allow us to further our interests and tighten our grip on global sectors."

Clara looked uneasy. "Isn't that risky? What if we're exposed?"

Victor's eyes glinted with mischief. "That's the beauty of it. The world is so desperate for corporate entities to support their causes that they'll overlook the finer details. All we need to do is play our cards right."

Raymond nodded, impressed. "It's a brilliant strategy. Use the public's passion for change to our advantage."

Victor raised his glass, "To controlling the narrative and furthering our global dominance."

The room echoed with the clinking of glasses, but Clara remained silent, her thoughts swirling. She had joined BlackStone believing in its potential to make a positive impact. But now, she wondered if she was just a pawn in a much larger, darker game.

Distraction and Diversion

In a dimly lit, soundproof room deep within BlackStone's headquarters, a team of their best PR specialists and strategists convened for a confidential meeting. The walls were adorned with screens displaying real-time news feeds and social media trends from around the world. At the center stood a holographic table, projecting data analytics and sentiment analysis graphs.

Helena, the head of PR, paced the room, her stilettos clicking against the marble floor. "We've got a situation," she began, her voice dripping with urgency. "Our recent acquisition in the Amazon rainforest is about to go public. The environmentalists will have a field day."

A strategist, Marco, chimed in, "We need a diversion. Something that will capture the public's attention and divert it from our activities in the Amazon."

Helena nodded, "Exactly. And what better way than to champion a 'woke' cause? The world is hungry for corporate responsibility. We give them what they want, and in return, they turn a blind eye to our other activities."

A young analyst, Mia, hesitated before speaking, "But which cause? There are so many."

Helena smirked, "That's the beauty of it. We don't need to genuinely support any cause. We just need to make a loud enough noise. Organize a few events, donate to a couple of charities, get some celebrities on board. The media will lap it up."

Marco added, "And while the world is busy applauding our 'commitment' to social justice, we can continue our operations in the Amazon undisturbed."

Mia looked troubled, "Isn't that... unethical?"

Helena leaned in, her eyes cold, "Dear Mia, in this game, ethics is a luxury. Our goal is global dominance. And to achieve that, we must be willing to make sacrifices."

Marco nodded in agreement, "Distraction and diversion, that's how we've always operated. And it's worked wonders for us."

As the meeting concluded, Mia left the room with a heavy heart. She had always believed in the power of 'woke' movements to bring about positive change. But now, she realized that for companies like BlackStone, it was just another tool in their arsenal, a means to an end in their relentless pursuit of global dominance.

The Smoke and Mirrors Tactic

In the heart of New York City, atop a skyscraper that pierced the heavens, sat the opulent boardroom of BlackStone. The room was a testament to their wealth and influence, with panoramic views of the city and a long mahogany table that gleamed under the chandeliers. The room was abuzz with anticipation as the board members gathered for their quarterly review.

As the members settled into their plush leather chairs, a large screen at the head of the table flickered to life. It showcased a montage of BlackStone's recent social justice initiatives: building schools in impoverished areas, funding clean water projects in Africa, and supporting women's rights movements globally. The board members exchanged satisfied glances, their public image was impeccable.

However, as the screen darkened, the atmosphere in the room shifted. The real meeting was about to begin.

A senior executive, Mr. Donovan, stood up, adjusting his tie. "Ladies and gentlemen, while the world is busy singing our praises, it's time for us to focus on our next strategic move."

He clicked a button, and a new set of images appeared on the screen. They depicted vast tracts of land, mineral-rich mountains, and bustling local communities. "These are the regions where we've launched our social justice initiatives," Donovan explained. "And while the world sees our charitable endeavors, what they don't see is the goldmine of opportunities these regions present."

A board member, Ms. Lorraine, leaned forward, her interest piqued. "Are you suggesting we capitalize on these regions?"

Donovan smirked, "Precisely. Under the guise of our initiatives, we've gained unparalleled access to these areas. We can easily acquire land, tap into local resources, and even influence local politics."

Another member, Mr. Gupta, raised an eyebrow, "But won't that jeopardize our public image?"

Donovan chuckled, "That's the beauty of the smoke and mirrors tactic. As long as we continue our 'charitable' endeavors, the world will remain blind to our true intentions. We give them a feel-good story, and in return, we get a free pass."

Ms. Lorraine smiled, "It's brilliant. We not only consolidate power but also ensure that any criticism is immediately silenced by our 'good deeds'."

As the meeting continued, the board members discussed their plans in detail, each move meticulously calculated. The world might see BlackStone as champions of social justice, but behind closed doors, their true motives were clear. It was all a game of smoke and mirrors, a masterclass in misdirection, all in the name of global dominance.

Unveiling the Truth

In a dimly lit, underground chamber in BlackStone's headquarters, a select group of individuals gathered. This was no ordinary meeting room; it was a place where the company's most confidential strategies were discussed, away from prying eyes and ears. The walls, made of soundproof material, ensured that whatever was spoken within remained a secret.

At the head of the table sat Mr. Donovan, the senior executive, flanked by Ms. Lorraine and Mr. Gupta. The rest of the attendees were a mix of PR experts, social media influencers, and top-tier marketing strategists. The mood was tense, as everyone knew the gravity of the discussions that lay ahead.

Donovan cleared his throat, "We've done an excellent job in aligning ourselves with the 'woke' movement. The world sees us as champions of social justice. But we all know the truth. It's time to discuss our next steps."

A PR expert, Ms. Clarke, projected a series of graphs and charts onto a screen. "Our 'woke' campaigns have been immensely successful. Public sentiment towards BlackStone has never been more positive. However, we've noticed a few investigative journalists digging deeper, trying to uncover our true motives."

Mr. Gupta frowned, "We can't let them jeopardize our plans. What's our strategy?"

Ms. Lorraine smirked, "We continue the charade. We amplify our 'woke' campaigns, drowning out any negative press with an overwhelming amount of positive stories. We need to control the narrative."

A social media influencer, Mr. Reyes, chimed in, "I can rally my network. We can flood the internet with stories of BlackStone's philanthropy, ensuring that any dissenting voices are lost in the noise."

Donovan nodded in approval, "Excellent. We need to be relentless. Remember, our 'woke' alignment isn't just about looking good. It's about ensuring that we remain in a position of power, unchallenged."

As the meeting progressed, the group brainstormed ways to further weaponize the 'woke' ideology. From funding documentaries that showcased their 'commitment' to social justice to partnering with celebrities for high-profile campaigns, no stone was left unturned.

As the attendees left the chamber, the truth was clear. BlackStone's 'woke' posturing was a meticulously crafted facade, a means to an end. Beneath the veneer of social justice advocacy lay a cold, calculated strategy, all aimed at furthering their relentless pursuit of power and dominance. The world might be enamored by their 'woke' image, but behind the scenes, the true nature of their ambitions was all too evident.

Chapter 5
The Energy Crisis Conundrum: A Calculated Play

The Global Energy Landscape and BlackStone's Role

The sun was setting over the sprawling cityscape, casting long shadows over the towering skyscrapers. In one of the penthouses of the city's most luxurious buildings, a group of influential individuals gathered around a polished mahogany table. The room was filled with the soft hum of conversation, punctuated by the clinking of glasses. Expensive artwork adorned the walls, and a large window offered a panoramic view of the city below.

At the head of the table sat Mr. Harrison, BlackStone's Director of Energy Investments. Flanking him were Ms. Valentina, an expert in renewable energy, and Mr. Chen, a mogul in the oil industry. The rest of the attendees were a mix of energy analysts, lobbyists, and representatives from major energy corporations.

Harrison raised his glass for a toast, "To a world in flux and the opportunities it presents." The sentiment was echoed by the attendees, their faces a mix of anticipation and greed.

Valentina, with her sharp features and piercing eyes, began the discussion. "The energy sector is in disarray. Renewable energy sources are gaining traction, but fossil fuels still dominate. The market is volatile, and prices are soaring."

Chen, stroking his beard thoughtfully, added, "And amidst this chaos, there's an opportunity for us to not just profit but to control. The world is desperate for stability, and we can provide that, for a price."

Harrison leaned forward, his eyes scanning the room. "BlackStone has always been at the forefront of global shifts. This energy crisis is no different. We have the resources, the connections, and the expertise to not just navigate these turbulent waters but to steer the ship."

An energy analyst, Dr. Ramirez, projected a series of graphs onto a screen. "Our research indicates that while there's a push for green energy, the world is still heavily reliant on oil and gas. If we can control the supply lines, dictate prices, and influence policy decisions, we can ensure that BlackStone remains not just a player but the puppet master."

Valentina smirked, "And with the current geopolitical tensions, countries are more inclined to secure their energy sources. We can broker deals, ensuring that nations dance to our tune."

Chen nodded in agreement, "We've already started making strategic investments in key regions. From oil fields in the Middle East to solar farms in Africa, BlackStone is positioning itself to be the energy kingpin."

As the evening progressed, the group discussed intricate strategies, from influencing global energy policies to manipulating market dynamics. The goal was clear: to ensure that BlackStone emerged as the dominant force in the global energy landscape.

As the attendees left the penthouse, the city lights below shimmered like a sea of stars. But above, in that room, a plan was set in motion, one that would see BlackStone not just observing the global energy shifts but possibly orchestrating them for their dark ambitions.

Divestment from High-Carbon Investments:
A Double-Edged Sword

The sun had barely risen, casting a soft golden hue over the city. In a discreet corner of an upscale café, two individuals sat across from each other, nursing their coffees. One was Elise, a seasoned journalist known for her investigative pieces, and the other was a shadowy figure known only as "The Informant."

Elise, her brow furrowed, began, "I've been tracking BlackStone's investments for years. Their sudden divestment from high-carbon assets seemed... out of character. It's as if they're trying to paint themselves as the good guys."

The Informant, a man with deep-set eyes and an air of mystery, replied, "It's all a game, Elise. On the surface, it looks like they're championing the environment. But if you dig deeper, you'll see the ripples their actions have caused."

Elise leaned in, intrigued. "Go on."

The Informant took a sip of his coffee, his gaze unwavering. "By pulling out of high-carbon investments, BlackStone created a vacuum. Smaller, less regulated entities rushed in to fill the gap, leading to even more environmental degradation and market instability. It's chaos out there."

Elise's eyes widened. "So, you're saying BlackStone's move wasn't about saving the planet?"

The Informant chuckled, "Far from it. By creating market gaps, they've made these assets more valuable. They can now re-enter the market, buying them at a fraction of the cost. It's a classic pump-and-dump strategy, but on a global scale."

Elise jotted down notes, her mind racing. "But why? Why go through all this trouble?"

The Informant leaned in, his voice barely above a whisper. "Control, Elise. By destabilizing the market, they can dictate terms, set prices, and essentially hold nations hostage to their energy needs. It's a power play, hidden behind a mask of environmental concern."

Elise looked up, realization dawning on her. "So, the divestment was just a smokescreen?"

The Informant nodded, "Exactly. And while the world applauds BlackStone for their 'green' initiatives, they're silently tightening their grip on the global energy sector."

The two continued their conversation, with Elise gathering as much information as she could. As the café began to fill up, The Informant stood up, leaving a small envelope on the table. "Everything you need is in there. Be careful, Elise. They're watching."

Elise watched him leave, the weight of the information heavy on her shoulders. BlackStone's divestment from high-carbon investments was not a noble endeavor but a calculated move with a hidden agenda. The challenge now was to unveil the truth to the world.

The Vacuum Effect and Market Chaos

The grand ballroom of the Ritz-Carlton was abuzz with chatter. Industry leaders, energy experts, and influential policymakers had gathered for the annual Global Energy Summit. Among the attendees was Victor Hale, a seasoned energy analyst with over two decades of experience. As he sipped his champagne, his eyes darted around the room, observing the power dynamics at play.

A familiar voice interrupted his thoughts. "Victor! Long time no see!" It was Clara, an old colleague and now a senior executive at a leading energy firm.

Victor smiled, "Clara! Always a pleasure. How have you been navigating these turbulent times?"

Clara sighed, "It's been a rollercoaster. Ever since BlackStone pulled out of the high-carbon sector, the market's been in chaos. Smaller firms are scrambling to fill the void, but it's like trying to plug a dam with a finger."

Victor nodded, "The vacuum effect. BlackStone's absence has destabilized the sector. Prices are fluctuating wildly, and there's a sense of unpredictability."

Clara leaned in, her voice dropping to a whisper, "But here's the kicker. Rumor has it that BlackStone is waiting in the wings, ready to swoop in and capitalize on the chaos they've created."

Victor raised an eyebrow, intrigued. "So, they create a void, watch the market spiral, and then...?"

Clara finished his sentence, "...And then they re-enter, buying assets at rock-bottom prices. It's genius, in a diabolical sort of way."

Victor pondered this revelation. "It's a classic strategy. Create a problem and then offer the solution. But on such a grand scale? It's audacious."

Clara smirked, "That's BlackStone for you. Always several steps ahead."

The two continued discussing the implications of BlackStone's maneuvers. As the evening wore on, Victor couldn't shake off a nagging feeling. The energy sector was a lifeline for countless nations, and BlackStone's manipulations could have far-reaching consequences.

As the summit concluded, Victor made a decision. He would delve deeper into BlackStone's strategies, hoping to unravel their intricate web of deceit. The vacuum effect was just the tip of the iceberg, and he was determined to expose the full extent of the market chaos BlackStone had orchestrated.

Political Puppetry: BlackStone's Influence Over Policy

The sun was setting over the city, casting a golden hue on the iconic Capitol Building. Inside, Senator Richard Mitchell was in his office, pouring over a stack of energy policy proposals. His assistant, a young woman named Emily, knocked softly and entered.

"Senator, you have a visitor. Mr. Adrian Kane from BlackStone," she announced, a hint of unease in her voice.

Mitchell looked up, his expression hardening. "Send him in."

Adrian Kane, a tall man with sharp features and an air of confidence, strolled in. "Senator Mitchell," he greeted with a sly smile, extending his hand.

"Mr. Kane," Mitchell responded coolly, shaking his hand briefly. "To what do I owe the pleasure?"

Kane took a seat, leaning back comfortably. "I wanted to discuss the upcoming energy policies. BlackStone believes there are... adjustments that could benefit both the nation and the market."

Mitchell raised an eyebrow. "Adjustments?"

Kane slid a folder across the table. "Just a few suggestions. We believe these policies could stabilize the energy sector."

Mitchell skimmed through the documents, his face betraying no emotion. "These policies seem to favor certain... corporate entities."

Kane chuckled. "It's a win-win, Senator. The nation gets stability, and businesses thrive."

Emily, who had been silent till now, interjected, "But at what cost? These policies could lead to further monopolization, concentrating power in the hands of a few."

Kane shot her a cold glance. "It's about efficiency, Ms...?"

"Emily," she responded defiantly.

"Efficiency, Ms. Emily. Consolidation leads to streamlined operations and better management."

Mitchell leaned forward, locking eyes with Kane. "Or it leads to manipulation and unchecked power. BlackStone's influence in the political sphere is becoming a concern."

Kane smirked, "Influence is just a tool, Senator. It's how you wield it that matters."

The room was thick with tension. Mitchell finally spoke, "I'll consider your suggestions, Mr. Kane. But remember, the interests of the nation come first."

Kane stood up, adjusting his tie. "Of course, Senator. We're all patriots here." With a final nod, he left the room.

Emily turned to Mitchell, "You're not seriously considering his proposals, are you?"

Mitchell sighed, "BlackStone's reach is vast, Emily. But we have a duty to the people. We'll tread carefully."

As the night deepened, the two delved into the policy suggestions, determined to decipher BlackStone's true intentions. The game of political puppetry had begun, and the stakes were higher than ever.

The Green Agenda or a Smokescreen?

The annual Global Sustainability Summit was in full swing, with leaders and influencers from around the world gathered in a grand hall adorned with green banners and eco-friendly displays. The atmosphere was electric, filled with hope and determination to combat the pressing environmental challenges.

Amidst the crowd, two journalists, Clara and Raj, stood observing the attendees. Clara, with her sharp eyes and notebook in hand, remarked, "Look at the BlackStone delegation. They're certainly making their presence felt."

Raj, sipping his organic tea, replied, "It's interesting, isn't it? A few years ago, they wouldn't be caught dead at an event like this. Now, they're parading around as the champions of sustainability."

Clara nodded, "It's a smart move, aligning with the green agenda. But I can't help but wonder if it's all for show."

Just then, a voice interrupted their conversation. "Wondering about BlackStone's intentions, are we?" It was Dr. Helena Foster, a renowned environmental scientist known for her candid views.

Clara smiled, "Dr. Foster! Always a pleasure. And yes, we were just discussing BlackStone's sudden interest in sustainability."

Dr. Foster adjusted her glasses, "It's a double-edged sword. On one hand, their investments in renewable energy and green technologies are commendable. But on the other, one can't help but question the motives behind such a drastic shift."

Raj interjected, "You mean it could be a smokescreen?"

Dr. Foster nodded, "Exactly. While they're out here shaking hands and making green pledges, what's happening behind closed doors? Are they genuinely committed to the cause, or is this just a strategic move to divert attention from other, less savory activities?"

Clara looked thoughtful, "It's a complex web. But if BlackStone's green agenda is just a facade, what are they trying to hide?"

Dr. Foster sighed, "That's the million-dollar question. But remember, in the world of global finance and power plays, things are rarely as they seem."

The trio continued their discussion, delving deeper into the intricacies of BlackStone's actions. As the summit progressed, it became clear that while the world celebrated BlackStone's green initiatives, discerning eyes remained watchful, determined to unveil the truth behind the smokescreen.

Profiting from Chaos: BlackStone's Calculated Play

The sun was setting over the sprawling cityscape, casting a golden hue over the towering skyscrapers. Inside one of the city's most exclusive bars, a group of business magnates gathered, their conversations a mix of business and pleasure. At the center of it all was Victor Hale, a top executive at BlackStone, known for his cunning strategies and ruthless ambition.

"To chaos," Victor toasted, raising his glass of aged whiskey.

A fellow magnate, Isabella, smirked, "And to profiting from it."

Victor took a sip, savoring the taste. "The energy market is in disarray, and while the world scrambles, we at BlackStone see a golden opportunity."

Isabella leaned in, her interest piqued. "Do tell."

Victor's eyes gleamed with mischief. "It's simple, really. As countries grapple with energy shortages and rising prices, they become desperate for solutions. And who better to provide those solutions than BlackStone?"

Across the room, a young journalist named Leo eavesdropped on the conversation, his instincts telling him he was onto something big.

Isabella laughed, "So, while the world sees a crisis, you see dollar signs?"

Victor nodded, "Precisely. We've strategically positioned ourselves in renewable energy sectors, battery technologies, and even in traditional oil and gas. No matter which way the wind blows, BlackStone stands to profit."

Leo discreetly jotted down notes, realizing the gravity of what he was uncovering. BlackStone wasn't just a passive observer in the energy crisis; they were actively shaping it to their advantage.

Isabella raised an eyebrow, "But isn't there a risk? What if global policies shift or if there's a backlash against companies seen as profiteering from the crisis?"

Victor smirked, "That's the beauty of it. We've got our hands in every pie. Whether it's lobbying for favorable policies or influencing public opinion, BlackStone is always several steps ahead."

The evening wore on, but Leo had heard enough. He slipped out of the bar, determined to expose BlackStone's calculated play. As he walked into the night, he realized the depth of BlackStone's influence. They weren't just capitalizing on the crisis; they were orchestrating it, turning global concerns into a chessboard where they held all the pieces.

The Bigger Picture: Power, Control, and Global Dominance

In a dimly lit, opulent boardroom at the top of BlackStone's headquarters, the company's inner circle convened. The room, adorned with rare art pieces and a panoramic view of the city, was a symbol of their vast wealth and influence. At the head of the long mahogany table sat Lawrence, the enigmatic mastermind behind BlackStone's meteoric rise.

"Colleagues," Lawrence began, his voice dripping with authority, "we stand on the cusp of a new era. An era where BlackStone doesn't just participate in the global narrative but dictates it."

A murmur of agreement rippled through the room. Eleanor, a shrewd strategist known for her analytical prowess, projected a world map on the screen. "As you can see, our influence in the energy sector now spans continents. From oil fields in the Middle East to solar farms in Africa, we have assets everywhere."

Lawrence nodded, "And with the current energy crisis, nations are looking to us for solutions. Solutions that we can provide, at a price."

A younger executive, Damien, leaned forward, "But it's not just about the money, is it?"

Lawrence smiled, a cold, calculating smile. "No, Damien. Money is just a tool. What we seek is power. The kind of power that allows us to shape global policies, influence nations, and control the very fabric of society."

Eleanor clicked to the next slide, showing graphs of BlackStone's projected growth. "With the current trajectory, we're not just looking at increased profits. We're looking at unparalleled dominance. A world where BlackStone's word is law."

Damien, still trying to grasp the enormity of their plans, asked, "And what's the endgame?"

Lawrence leaned back, steepling his fingers. "Complete and utter control. A world where every major decision, be it economic, political, or social, has BlackStone's fingerprints on it."

The room was silent, the weight of Lawrence's words sinking in. They weren't just playing a game; they were crafting a new world order.

As the meeting adjourned, the executives left the room, each absorbed in their thoughts. The energy crisis was just a steppingstone, a means to an end. And as the world grappled with power outages and soaring prices, BlackStone was positioning itself as the puppet master, pulling the strings of global destiny.

Chapter 6
The Chinese Connection: A Dance with the Dragon

Setting the Stage: BlackStone and the CCP

In the heart of Beijing, nestled amidst ancient temples and sprawling skyscrapers, lies a discreet building known only to the elite. It's here, away from prying eyes, that the most confidential of meetings occur. On a chilly winter evening, a sleek black limousine pulled up to this building. Out stepped Lawrence, BlackStone's enigmatic leader, flanked by his trusted advisors.

Greeting him was Minister Li, a high-ranking official of the Chinese Communist Party (CCP) and a key player in China's economic strategies. Their handshake, firm, and lingering was a testament to the deep-rooted ties between BlackStone and the CCP.

"Lawrence," Minister Li began as they walked through the ornate corridors adorned with Ming dynasty art, "it's been too long. Our last meeting in Shanghai was quite... productive."

Lawrence chuckled, "Indeed, Minister. The fusion of BlackStone's global reach with China's ambitions has been... mutually beneficial."

As they settled into a private chamber, a pot of aged pu'er tea was poured, its aroma filling the room. Minister Li took a moment, sipping the tea, before delving into the heart of the matter. "Our collaboration has been fruitful, but the world is changing rapidly. The West grows wary of China's rise, and we need allies, powerful allies like BlackStone."

Lawrence nodded, swirling the tea in his cup. "And the allure of the Chinese market, with its vast consumer base and untapped potential, is too tempting for BlackStone to ignore. Our interests align, Minister."

Minister Li leaned forward, his eyes sharp. "But it's not just about business, is it, Lawrence? This alliance, this dance with the dragon, it's about reshaping the global order."

Lawrence met his gaze, the weight of their shared vision palpable in the room. "Indeed. Together, we can craft a new narrative, one where East meets West, not as adversaries, but as partners."

The evening wore on as they discussed strategies, mergers, and global politics. It was clear that the relationship between BlackStone and the CCP was more than just business. It was a strategic alliance, born out of mutual ambitions and the allure of shared power.

As Lawrence left the building, the Beijing skyline glittering in the distance, he reflected on the partnership. The world was their chessboard, and together with the CCP, BlackStone was poised to make its next move.

The Mutual Gains: Access and Influence

In the bustling metropolis of Shanghai, the towering BlackStone headquarters stood as a testament to its growing influence in the East. Inside, a state-of-the-art conference room was abuzz with activity. Executives from both BlackStone and various Chinese conglomerates were gathered, poring over charts, graphs, and projections.

"By partnering with us," began Zhang Wei, a top executive from one of China's leading tech firms, "BlackStone gains unparalleled access to the Chinese market. Think of the potential consumer base, the emerging technologies, the infrastructure projects!"

Lawrence, ever the astute businessman, nodded appreciatively. "And in return, the CCP gets a foot in the door of our vast global networks. From Wall Street to European capitals, our reach is extensive."

A CCP official, Madame Liu, elegantly dressed and with an air of authority, chimed in, "It's not just about business, Lawrence. It's about influence.

With BlackStone by our side, we can navigate the complexities of global politics more effectively. Your connections in the West are invaluable."

Lawrence leaned back, taking a moment to absorb the weight of Madame Liu's words. "True, Madame Liu. But let's not forget the risks. The West is wary of China's growing influence. Our alliance, while beneficial, will be under constant scrutiny."

Madame Liu smiled enigmatically. "Every great venture comes with its challenges. But together, we can overcome them."

As the meeting progressed, it became evident that the alliance was more than just a business partnership. It was a symbiotic relationship, with both parties feeding off each other's strengths. BlackStone's entry into the Chinese market meant tapping into a goldmine of opportunities, from tech startups to massive infrastructure projects. On the other hand, the CCP, with its newfound access to BlackStone's global networks, could extend its influence far beyond its borders.

Over a lavish dinner that evening, Lawrence found himself seated next to an old friend, James, a journalist with deep insights into global geopolitics. "This alliance of yours," James began, swirling his wine, "it's a game-changer. But you must be careful. The world is watching."

Lawrence smirked, "Isn't that the point, James? To be at the center of it all?"

James raised an eyebrow, "Just remember, with great power comes great responsibility. And sometimes, a hefty price."

The night wore on, filled with laughter, clinking glasses, and hushed conversations. But beneath the revelry, the wheels of strategy and influence were in constant motion. The alliance between BlackStone and the CCP was not just about mutual gains; it was a dance of power, with each partner trying to lead.

The Darker Side: Endorsing Authoritarianism

In a dimly lit, upscale bar in Beijing, two figures sat in a secluded corner, their conversation barely audible over the soft jazz playing in the background. One was an investigative journalist, Li Wei, known for his fearless exposés on the CCP's controversial practices. The other was a former BlackStone executive, Alex, who had left the company under mysterious circumstances.

Li Wei took a sip of his drink, his eyes scanning the room cautiously. "You know, Alex, when I first heard about BlackStone's alliance with the CCP, I was intrigued. But the more I dug, the more I realized the gravity of this partnership."

Alex leaned in, his voice low. "BlackStone's association with the CCP isn't just about business, Li. It's an implicit endorsement of the party's practices. The surveillance, the censorship, the human rights abuses – by aligning with them, BlackStone is turning a blind eye to it all."

Li Wei's eyes darkened. "I've seen firsthand the lengths the party will go to suppress dissent. Friends, colleagues... they've disappeared, silenced for speaking out. And now, with BlackStone in the picture, I fear the situation will only worsen."

Alex sighed, rubbing his temples. "When I was with BlackStone, there were whispers. Whispers about the company's involvement in surveillance tech projects, about data-sharing agreements that would bolster the CCP's control over its citizens. I couldn't be a part of it anymore."

Li Wei looked at Alex, admiration evident in his eyes. "It takes courage to walk away from such power, Alex. But what can we do? How can we expose the truth behind this alliance?"

Alex leaned back, a determined look on his face. "We gather evidence, build a case. With your contacts and my insider knowledge, we can shed light on BlackStone's ethical compromises."

The two men sat in silence for a moment, the weight of their mission pressing down on them. The alliance between BlackStone and the CCP was more than just a business venture; it was a dangerous liaison with far-reaching implications. By endorsing the CCP's authoritarian practices, BlackStone was playing a high-stakes game, one that could have dire consequences for the very fabric of global democracy.

As the night wore on, Li Wei and Alex plotted their next moves, determined to unveil the truth behind BlackStone's dark alliance. The dance with the dragon had begun, and the world was watching.

The Price of Partnership: Overlooking Human Rights Abuses

In a sprawling penthouse overlooking Shanghai's skyline, BlackStone's senior executives gathered for a confidential meeting. The room was filled with tension, the air thick with anticipation. At the head of the table sat Richard, BlackStone's Vice President of Asian Operations, a man known for his ruthless pragmatism.

"As you all know," Richard began, his voice cold and measured, "our partnership with the CCP has been immensely profitable. Our foothold in the Chinese market has never been stronger."

A younger executive, Clara, hesitated before speaking up. "But at what cost, Richard? Every day, there are reports of the CCP's human rights abuses. The internment camps, the suppression of free speech, the crackdown on Hong Kong. How can we, in good conscience, continue to align ourselves with such a regime?"

Richard's eyes narrowed, his gaze piercing. "Our primary responsibility is to our shareholders, Clara. Profit is the bottom line. The political intricacies of our partners are not our concern."

Clara's face flushed with anger. "But there's a line, Richard! A line between business and basic human decency. Are we really willing to overlook the suffering of millions for the sake of our balance sheets?"

A murmur of agreement rippled through the room. Many of the executives had been grappling with the same moral dilemma.

Richard leaned forward, his voice dripping with condescension. "Clara, we live in a world of realpolitik. Idealism is a luxury we cannot afford. Our alliance with the CCP is strategic, and we must prioritize our company's interests."

Another executive, Raj, chimed in, "But Richard, our reputation is at stake. The global community is watching. If we continue to turn a blind eye to the CCP's transgressions, we risk alienating our stakeholders and tarnishing our brand."

Richard smirked, "Let them watch. We've weathered storms before. This is no different."

The room fell silent, the weight of the moral quandary palpable. The executives were torn between their duty to the company and their personal ethics. The price of partnership with the CCP was becoming increasingly clear: a willingness to overlook grave human rights abuses for the sake of profit.

As the meeting adjourned, Clara and Raj exchanged a determined glance. They knew they had to take a stand, even if it meant going against the company's top brass. The dance with the dragon was proving to be more treacherous than they had ever imagined.

A New World Order: The CCP's Global Vision

In the heart of Beijing, within the ornate halls of the Forbidden City, a clandestine meeting was underway. The room was dimly lit, its walls adorned with ancient tapestries that whispered tales of China's glorious past. At the center of a long mahogany table sat General Li, a high-ranking CCP official, and across from him was Mr. Thornton, BlackStone's Chief Strategy Officer.

General Li poured tea for both of them, the aroma filling the room. "Mr. Thornton," he began, his voice deep and resonant, "China has always been a civilization with a grand vision. For millennia, we've been at the center of the world's stage. Now, with the dawn of a new era, we seek to reclaim that position."

Mr. Thornton nodded, intrigued. "And how does BlackStone fit into this vision, General?"

General Li leaned back, his eyes gleaming with ambition. "The world is changing, Mr. Thornton. The West's influence is waning, and the East is rising. We see a new world order on the horizon, one where China is the dominant force. But to achieve this, we need allies. Allies with influence, reach, and power. Allies like BlackStone."

Mr. Thornton sipped his tea, processing the gravity of General Li's words. "And what would this partnership entail?"

General Li smiled, revealing a hint of cunning. "A symbiotic relationship. BlackStone provides us with the financial muscle and global networks we need to expand our influence. In return, we offer you unparalleled access to the vast opportunities within China and beyond."

As the conversation deepened, it became clear that the CCP's global vision was not just about economic dominance. It was about reshaping the world's political and cultural landscape, with China at its helm. And BlackStone, with its vast resources and global reach, was the perfect vehicle to help realize this vision.

Mr. Thornton, ever the pragmatist, saw the potential benefits for BlackStone. "This could be a game-changer for us," he mused. "But it's not without risks. Aligning ourselves so closely with the CCP could draw scrutiny and backlash."

General Li chuckled, "Every great endeavor comes with risks, Mr. Thornton. But the rewards? They are beyond your wildest dreams."

As the meeting concluded, the two men shook hands, sealing a partnership that would reshape the world's geopolitical landscape. The dance with the dragon had taken a new turn, one that promised power and influence but also carried the weight of immense responsibility and potential peril.

The Global Implications:
Power Dynamics and Future Concerns

In a luxurious penthouse overlooking the New York skyline, a group of world leaders, influential business magnates, and policy experts gathered for an emergency summit. The topic of discussion? The burgeoning alliance between BlackStone and the CCP and its potential ramifications on the global stage.

As the attendees settled into their seats, the room buzzed with hushed conversations. The atmosphere was thick with tension, a testament to the gravity of the situation. Sir Richard Harlow, a renowned geopolitical analyst, took the podium, his sharp eyes scanning the room.

"Ladies and gentlemen," he began, "we stand at a pivotal moment in history. The alliance between BlackStone and the CCP isn't just a business deal; it's a seismic shift in global power dynamics."

A murmur of agreement rippled through the room. Maria Gonzales, the CEO of a major European bank, raised her hand. "Sir Harlow, while we understand the potential economic implications, what concerns me is the political and social fallout. How will this alliance impact democratic values, human rights, and global governance?"

Sir Harlow nodded, acknowledging her concerns. "Excellent question, Ms. Gonzales. By aligning with the CCP, BlackStone is indirectly endorsing an authoritarian regime. This could embolden other nations to adopt similar models, undermining democratic institutions worldwide."

A hush fell over the room as the weight of his words sank in. Akio Tanaka, a tech mogul from Japan, chimed in, "And what about the technological implications? With BlackStone's vast resources and the CCP's technological prowess, they could potentially control global data flows, surveillance systems, and even the future of AI."

Sir Harlow agreed, "Indeed, Mr. Tanaka. The fusion of BlackStone's financial might with the CCP's technological advancements could lead to a new era of digital authoritarianism. International stakeholders must be vigilant."

As the discussion continued, it became evident that the alliance's implications extended far beyond economics. The very fabric of global society was at stake. From concerns about data privacy and surveillance to fears of a new Cold War, the partnership between BlackStone and the CCP was a game-changer.

Lena Ivanova, a human rights activist from Russia, voiced her concerns. "We've seen the CCP's human rights abuses firsthand. By partnering with them, BlackStone risks becoming complicit in these violations. The world must hold them accountable."

The summit concluded with a call to action. The attendees recognized the need for a united front to address the challenges posed by the BlackStone-CCP alliance. As they departed, they were acutely aware that the future was uncertain, and the stakes had never been higher. The dance with the dragon had global implications, and the world was watching closely.

The Final Verdict: A Dance of Ambition and Dominance

In a dimly lit, opulent room adorned with ancient Chinese tapestries and modern art, two figures sat across from each other, separated only by a mahogany table. On one side was Jonathan Hale, BlackStone's enigmatic vice president, and on the other, General Li Wei, a high-ranking official within the CCP. The ambiance was thick with anticipation, the silence only broken by the occasional clink of a teacup.

General Li took a deliberate sip of his tea, his eyes never leaving Hale's. "Mr. Hale," he began in a measured tone, "our nations have had their differences, but our organizations see the world similarly. Power, control, dominance. These are not just words; they are philosophies."

Hale leaned back, intertwining his fingers. "General Li, BlackStone has always believed in strategic partnerships. Our alliance with the CCP is not just about business; it's about reshaping the global order. Together, we can redefine the future."

Li Wei smirked, "A future where BlackStone and the CCP stand at the helm?"

Hale nodded, "Precisely. A dance of ambition and dominance. While the world remains preoccupied with trivial matters, we can pull the strings from the shadows."

The conversation shifted to the intricacies of their partnership. From investments in cutting-edge technology to influencing global policies, the duo discussed their shared vision. It was clear that this wasn't a mere business transaction; it was a union of two powerhouses with a shared goal of global supremacy.

As the evening wore on, the two men delved deeper into their plans. They spoke of leveraging BlackStone's financial might with the CCP's political influence, creating a synergy that would be unstoppable. The world was their chessboard, and they were positioning themselves to be the ultimate victors.

Outside the room, a young aide eavesdropped, her heart racing. She had heard rumors of this alliance, but the reality was far more chilling. The sheer audacity of their ambitions was staggering. She realized that this wasn't just a dance; it was a meticulously choreographed ballet of power and control.

As the meeting concluded, Hale and Li Wei exchanged a firm handshake, sealing their pact. The world remained oblivious to the storm brewing on the horizon. But one thing was clear: BlackStone's dance with the dragon was more than just a partnership; it was a declaration of their intent to dominate the global stage.

Chapter 7
Media Puppeteers: Crafting the Global Narrative

The Power of Narrative: Setting the Stage

The dim glow of a television screen illuminated a room, casting shadows on the faces of the family gathered around it. News anchors, with their polished appearances and rehearsed tones, delivered stories from around the globe. To the average viewer, it was just another evening news segment. But behind the scenes, a more intricate plot was unfolding.

In a luxurious penthouse overlooking the city, Marcus Caldwell, BlackStone's Head of Media Relations, sat with a group of influential media moguls. The room was filled with the scent of expensive cigars and aged whiskey. Large screens displayed various news channels, each echoing a similar narrative.

"Media isn't just about reporting facts," Marcus began, swirling his drink. "It's about crafting a story, a narrative. And whoever controls that narrative, controls the world."

One of the moguls, a silver-haired woman named Eleanor, nodded in agreement. "People believe what they see and hear. They don't question the source. They don't dig deeper. And that's where our power lies."

A younger executive, visibly eager, chimed in, "So, we're not just reporting the news; we're creating it?"

Marcus smirked, "Precisely. Think of it as a play. We set the stage, choose the actors, and write the script. The world is our audience, and they're none the wiser."

The conversation shifted to BlackStone's investments in various media outlets. From newspapers to television networks, their reach was vast. By subtly influencing the content, they could steer public opinion in any direction they desired.

Eleanor leaned forward, her eyes sharp. "But we must be careful. The narrative should be seamless, consistent across all platforms. Any discrepancy, and we risk exposure."

Marcus nodded, "That's why we're here. To ensure our message is unified. BlackStone's vision for the future needs to be the world's vision."

As the evening progressed, the group discussed strategies to further their agenda. From highlighting certain global events while downplaying others to endorsing specific political candidates, the media was their most potent tool.

Outside the penthouse, a journalist stood, having caught snippets of the conversation. The weight of the revelation was overwhelming. The media, which was supposed to be the watchdog of society, was being manipulated by the very powers it was meant to keep in check.

The stage was set, and the players were in position. BlackStone's involvement in the media landscape wasn't just about business; it was about controlling the narrative, shaping perceptions, and ultimately, determining the course of global events.

BlackStone's Media Empire:
Strategic Investments and Alliances

The sun was setting over Manhattan, casting a golden hue over the skyscrapers. Inside a lavish boardroom adorned with mahogany and gold, BlackStone's top executives gathered around a large table. At the head sat Victor Hale, the company's Chief Strategy Officer, with a series of folders spread out before him. Each folder bore the logo of a different media company.

"As we all know," Victor began, adjusting his glasses, "the media is not just about news. It's about influence. And influence, gentlemen, is power."

A large screen behind him lit up, displaying a web of interconnected logos – CNN, BBC, Fox News, The New York Times, and many others. Lines connected them, indicating BlackStone's investments and stakes in each entity.

"Over the past decade," Victor continued, "we've strategically positioned ourselves within the media industry. From television networks to print media, from radio stations to online platforms, our reach is unparalleled."

A murmur of agreement spread across the room. One executive, a sharp-eyed woman named Isabella, raised her hand. "It's not just about ownership, Victor. It's about the alliances we've forged."

Victor nodded, "Indeed, Isabella. Our partnerships with influential media figures have been invaluable." He clicked a button, and the screen shifted to display images of prominent journalists, editors, and media moguls, many of whom had been seen at BlackStone's events or had personal ties to its executives.

A younger executive, Lucas, looked intrigued. "So, we're not just passive investors. We're actively shaping the content?"

Victor smirked, "Exactly. Think of it as guiding the narrative. We suggest they implement. A nudge here, a suggestion there, and the global conversation shifts in our favor."

Isabella chimed in, "And it's not just about what's reported, but how it's reported. The framing, the tone, the emphasis. It's all calculated."

Lucas, still trying to grasp the enormity of it all, asked, "But what about pushback? Surely, some journalists resist?"

Victor leaned back, a confident smile playing on his lips. "Ah, Lucas, that's where our alliances come into play. A journalist might resist, but what about their editor? Or the network's CEO? Or the major shareholder? Somewhere along the chain, our influence is felt."

The room grew silent, the weight of their influence palpable. They weren't just investors; they were puppeteers, pulling the strings of global media.

Outside the boardroom, a secretary named Clara overheard snippets of the conversation. She had always known BlackStone was powerful, but this? This was something else entirely. She realized that the news she consumed, the stories she read, were all part of a larger narrative, one crafted by the very company she worked for.

As the meeting adjourned, the executives left, confident in their control over the global narrative. But as the old adage goes, "Walls have ears." And in this case, those ears belonged to Clara, who now held a secret that could shake the very foundations of BlackStone's media empire.

Behind the Scenes: Collaborations and Control

The heart of New York City pulsed with life, its streets a cacophony of sounds and sights. But high above, in a penthouse suite overlooking Central Park, the atmosphere was decidedly different. The room, dimly lit by a single chandelier, was filled with a select group of individuals. These were not just any individuals; they were the titans of the media world - influential journalists, renowned editors, and powerful media moguls.

At the center of the room stood a grand oak table, and seated at its head was Adrian Kane, BlackStone's Director of Media Relations. His sharp features and piercing eyes gave him an air of authority. "Ladies and gentlemen," he began, his voice smooth and commanding, "I trust you understand why you're here."

A murmur of acknowledgment spread across the room. Everyone present was aware of their unique relationship with BlackStone. Some had received generous sponsorships for their programs, others had been offered exclusive stories, and a few had even been bailed out during financial crises.

Adrian continued, "We value our collaborations with each of you. But remember, collaboration is a two-way street." He paused, letting the implication of his words sink in. "We provide, and in return, we expect certain... narratives to be highlighted."

A journalist from a leading daily, known for his investigative pieces, cleared his throat. "Adrian, we appreciate BlackStone's support, but we have our journalistic integrity to maintain."

Adrian smiled, a cold, calculated smile. "Of course, Richard. We respect integrity. But let's not forget the bigger picture. Sometimes, certain stories, certain angles, are more... beneficial for all involved."

An editor from a prominent news network chimed in, "So, you're saying we should skew our stories to favor BlackStone?"

Adrian raised a hand, "Not skew, my dear. Just... prioritize. Highlight the positives, downplay the negatives. It's all about perspective."

A young media mogul, who had recently inherited a chain of magazines, looked uneasy. "And if we don't play by these rules?"

Adrian's gaze turned icy. "Then perhaps our collaboration comes to an end. And with it, all the benefits you've enjoyed."

The room grew tense. The power dynamics were clear. BlackStone held the cards, and they weren't afraid to play them.

As the meeting drew to a close, the media personalities left with a mix of emotions. Some felt compromised, others justified it as a necessary evil, and a few were simply indifferent. But one thing was clear: BlackStone's tentacles reached deep into the media world, ensuring that the stories that saw the light of day were ones that furthered their global ambitions.

Outside the penthouse, as the media moguls dispersed into the night, they carried with them the weight of their choices. To align with BlackStone's narrative or to risk it all for the sake of journalistic integrity? The battle between power and principle raged on.

The Endgame: Beyond Corporate Image Building

The sun had set over the city, casting long shadows over the skyscrapers. Inside a luxurious penthouse, a group of BlackStone's top executives gathered around a holographic table, displaying real-time data streams from various media outlets worldwide. The room was filled with a palpable tension, the kind that precedes significant decisions.

"Look at this," said Helena, BlackStone's Chief Strategy Officer, pointing to a cluster of news articles. "Our investments in renewable energy are getting positive coverage. The public sees us as pioneers in the green revolution."

Vincent, the Head of Public Relations, nodded in agreement. "Our PR campaigns have been successful, but we need to think bigger. It's not just about a positive corporate image anymore."

A third executive, Marcus, the Director of Global Operations, leaned forward, his fingers steepled. "Exactly. Image is just the tip of the iceberg. Our influence in the media can be a tool, a weapon even, to shape global narratives to our advantage."

Helena raised an eyebrow, intrigued. "Go on."

Marcus continued, "Consider this: if we can control the narrative around economic policies, political movements, even global crises, we can predict market movements, influence government decisions, and be always ten steps ahead."

Vincent chimed in, "Imagine the possibilities. We could endorse political candidates sympathetic to our interests, downplay economic crises in regions where we have significant investments, and even create demand for products before they hit the market."

Helena looked thoughtful. "So, you're suggesting we use our media influence not just for image building but as a chessboard for global dominance?"

Marcus nodded, "Precisely. We're not just playing the game; we're setting the rules."

A silence settled over the room as the magnitude of the idea sunk in. The potential was enormous, but so were the risks.

Suddenly, the door opened, and a young intern rushed in, holding a tablet. "Sorry to interrupt, but you need to see this." She played a clip of a renowned journalist exposing some of BlackStone's covert media operations.

The room's atmosphere turned icy. Helena's voice was sharp, "This is exactly why we need to be ahead. Control the narrative, control the game."

Vincent sighed, "It's a double-edged sword. The more we manipulate, the more scrutiny we invite."

Marcus looked determined, "Then let's ensure our moves are so subtle, so intricate, that even if someone catches a glimpse of our game, they can never see the full picture."

As the meeting adjourned, the executives left with a renewed sense of purpose. For BlackStone, the media wasn't just about shaping perceptions; it was about crafting a new world order, one where they held the reins of power. The endgame had begun.

Tactics and Suppression: Silencing the Dissent

In a dimly lit room, the walls adorned with screens displaying various news channels from around the world, sat a team of BlackStone's most skilled media strategists. Their task was clear: monitor, manipulate, and if necessary, muzzle any narrative that posed a threat to BlackStone's global ambitions.

A young analyst, Clara, pointed to a screen where a renowned investigative journalist was discussing BlackStone's questionable investments. "This is the third time this month he's gone after us. His following is growing."

A senior strategist, Mr. Reynolds, adjusted his glasses and said, "It's time we deal with him. Initiate a smear campaign. Dig into his past, find something, anything, that we can use to discredit him."

Another team member, Raj, chimed in, "We've tried that before. He's clean. But what if we shift the focus? Perhaps a scandal involving his family or close associates?"

Reynolds nodded, "Good. Create a diversion. And make sure it's sensational. The public has a short attention span; give them a new story to latch onto."

Clara hesitated, "But isn't that risky? What if it backfires?"

Reynolds smirked, "That's why we have contingency plans. If one narrative doesn't work, we flood the media with another. Confuse, distract, and dilute."

As the team got to work, another screen displayed a budding journalist from a small town, exposing BlackStone's attempts to buy out local media. Raj looked concerned, "She's gaining traction. Her story is trending."

Reynolds sighed, "Suppress it. Buy out her editors, offer them a price they can't refuse. If that doesn't work, threaten them with legal action. Most small outlets can't afford prolonged legal battles."

Clara looked troubled, "It feels...wrong. Silencing voices, manipulating truths."

Reynolds leaned in, his voice cold, "This is the price of dominance, Clara. In this world, it's eat or be eaten. And BlackStone does not intend to be on the menu."

As the day turned into night, the room buzzed with activity. Stories were altered, critics were silenced, and narratives were crafted. The puppeteers were at work, pulling the strings of global media, ensuring that the world saw only what BlackStone wanted them to see. The dance of deception was in full swing, and BlackStone was leading the waltz.

Crafting a World View: The Implications of Media Dominance

In a world where information is power, the ability to shape that information becomes the ultimate weapon. BlackStone, with its vast media empire, wielded this weapon with unparalleled precision. The implications of such dominance were far-reaching, touching every corner of the globe and every facet of society.

At a lavish penthouse overlooking the city, BlackStone's top executives gathered for a private dinner. The room was filled with the soft hum of conversation, punctuated by the clinking of glasses. At the head of the table, Helena, BlackStone's Chief Media Strategist, raised her glass for a toast. "To a world where every story is our story," she declared.

A murmur of agreement swept the room. Victor, a senior executive, leaned in, "It's fascinating, isn't it? We've managed to turn public opinion on its head. Wars, economic policies, even cultural shifts – all seen through the lens we provide."

Helena smirked, "And the beauty of it is, they believe it's their own perspective. Little do they realize that their 'opinions' are carefully crafted products of our design."

Across the table, a younger executive, Liam, looked thoughtful. "But what about the historians, the academics? Won't they see through our manipulations?"

Victor chuckled, "Ah, but history is written by the victors. And who's more victorious than us right now? Besides, academia isn't immune to our influence. A well-placed donation here, a scholarship there, and voilà – history starts to look a lot more...favorable."

Helena added, "And let's not forget the power of repetition. When every news outlet, every documentary, every article sings the same tune, it becomes the accepted truth. Over time, even the most discerning minds begin to accept it."

Liam frowned, "But isn't there a risk? What if people start to see through the facade?"

Helena's gaze turned icy, "That's why we stay ahead of the game. Control the dissent, amplify the distractions. Keep the masses entertained, and they won't have the time or inclination to question."

Victor nodded in agreement, "And if someone does manage to break through, well, there are ways to deal with them."

As the night wore on, the executives discussed their future plans, each more ambitious than the last. It was clear that BlackStone's media dominance wasn't just about profit; it was about reshaping the very fabric of society. By controlling the narrative, they controlled the world's perception of reality. And in doing so, they held the power to shape the future itself.

Conclusion: The Ultimate Weapon in the Quest for Dominance

In the vast tapestry of human history, few tools have held as much sway over the masses as the media. From the ancient bards who sang tales of heroes and gods to the modern newsrooms that broadcast events in real-time, the ability to control the narrative has always been a coveted power. And in the digital age, where information flows like water and opinions can be swayed with a single tweet, this power has reached its zenith.

In a dimly lit boardroom, high above the city's skyline, BlackStone's inner circle convened. The room, adorned with opulent art and state-of-the-art technology, was a testament to the company's vast wealth and influence. At the center, a holographic globe rotated, pinpointing BlackStone's media assets across continents.

"Information," began Cassandra, BlackStone's Director of Global Communications, "is no longer just about informing. It's about shaping, molding, and directing. With our assets, we don't just report the news; we create it."

A murmur of agreement rippled through the room. Marcus, a senior strategist, added, "And it's not just about the big stories. It's the subtle shifts, the nuances. Change the wording of a headline, emphasize one aspect over another, and you can change public sentiment overnight."

Aria, a digital media expert, chimed in, "And with the rise of social media algorithms, we can ensure that our narrative is the one that gets amplified. People believe they're making choices, but in reality, they're being fed a carefully curated stream of information."

Cassandra nodded, "Exactly. And it's not just about controlling what they see; it's about controlling how they feel. Fear, hope, anger, joy – these are the strings we pull to make the puppet dance."

The room fell silent for a moment, the weight of their influence palpable. Then, a voice from the back spoke up, "But what's the endgame? Is it just about profit?"

Cassandra smiled, a glint in her eye, "Profit is a means to an end. Our true goal is dominance. By controlling the narrative, we control perceptions. And by controlling perceptions, we control reality itself."

As the meeting adjourned, the members of BlackStone's inner circle left with a renewed sense of purpose. They understood that in the grand chessboard of global power dynamics, media was their queen – the most powerful piece, capable of moving in any direction and shaping the game's outcome. And with this weapon in their arsenal, BlackStone's quest for global dominance seemed not just plausible, but inevitable.

Introduction: The Dark Side of Corporate Advisories

In the sprawling metropolis of global business, towering skyscrapers and bustling boardrooms are the visible symbols of power and wealth. Yet, behind the polished marble lobbies and the gleaming glass facades, a shadowy world operates, where influence is peddled, and decisions are made that affect millions. At the heart of this world is BlackStone, a behemoth that doesn't just play the game but often dictates the rules.

The sun had barely risen over Manhattan, but the 50th-floor conference room in BlackStone's headquarters was already abuzz with activity. A group of sharply dressed executives gathered around a long mahogany table, each with a dossier in front of them. These were not just any dossiers; they were detailed profiles of companies BlackStone had significant stakes in.

"Alright, let's begin," said Victor Hale, BlackStone's Chief Advisory Strategist, his voice echoing slightly in the vast room. "We've got three companies on the agenda today. Let's start with the pharmaceuticals."

A screen at the end of the room lit up, displaying a logo of MedTech Corp, a leading pharmaceutical company. "Their new drug is showing promise," began Lydia, a senior analyst. "But there are side effects. Nothing fatal, but not entirely benign either."

Victor leaned back, steepling his fingers. "How can we spin this?"

A younger executive, James, cleared his throat. "We could emphasize the drug's benefits, downplay the side effects. Perhaps fund a few studies that highlight its positive impact?"

Victor nodded, "Good. And if any negative press emerges?"

"We have contacts in major health magazines," Lydia chimed in. "We can ensure that the narrative remains favorable."

The discussion moved on, but the pattern was clear. For BlackStone, it wasn't about the well-being of the consumers or ethical business practices. It was about control, influence, and, above all, profit.

As the hours ticked by, the group dissected company after company, crafting strategies, influencing decisions, and ensuring that BlackStone's interests were always paramount. To the outside world, these were just standard corporate practices, the usual ebb and flow of business. But those in the room knew better. They were orchestrating a symphony of manipulation, where the notes were companies, and the melody was BlackStone's ever-growing influence.

By the time the meeting concluded, the sun was setting, casting long shadows over the city. The executives left, confident in their plans, aware of the power they wielded. For in the world of corporate advisories, where profits often took precedence over people, BlackStone was the puppet master, pulling strings and shaping outcomes to fit their dark, ambitious narrative.

The Cost-Cutting Obsession: More Than Just Profits

In the vast, interconnected world of global business, the term 'cost-cutting' is often thrown around boardrooms like a golden mantra. It's seen as the key to leaner operations, higher profits, and increased shareholder value. But when BlackStone gets involved, cost-cutting takes on a more sinister hue.

The scene was a lavish penthouse suite in downtown New York, where BlackStone's top advisors were hosting a dinner for the CEOs of companies they had significant stakes in. The ambiance was opulent, with crystal chandeliers casting a soft glow over the room, and a private quartet playing a gentle serenade. But beneath the veneer of luxury, tension simmered.

As the main course was served, Helena Carter, BlackStone's Chief Financial Strategist, stood up, her red dress contrasting sharply against the muted tones of the room. "Ladies and gentlemen," she began, her voice dripping with charm, "we've invited you here tonight to discuss a matter of utmost importance: cost-cutting."

A murmur went through the room. Everyone knew BlackStone's reputation for aggressive cost-cutting, but hearing it discussed so openly was still jarring.

"Think of it as... streamlining," Helena continued, circling the room like a predator. "We believe there's always fat to trim. And when you cut down, you become leaner, more efficient, and ultimately, more profitable."

Robert Langley, the CEO of a tech startup, raised his hand hesitantly. "But at what cost? Last quarter, we had to lay off a significant portion of our workforce to meet your 'efficiency' targets. These were talented individuals who were with us from the beginning."

Helena smiled, but it didn't reach her eyes. "Sacrifices must be made, Robert. It's the nature of business."

But as the evening wore on, it became clear that BlackStone's cost-cutting obsession wasn't just about maximizing profits. It was a calculated strategy. By forcing companies to cut costs, BlackStone made them more vulnerable, often leading them to rely on BlackStone's vast resources to stay afloat. This dependency allowed BlackStone to exert even more control over their decisions, furthering their grip on the corporate world.

As dessert was served, a hush fell over the room. Helena raised her glass for a toast. "To efficiency, to profits, and to a brighter future under BlackStone's guidance."

The CEOs joined in, but their smiles were strained. They knew that in BlackStone's world, cost-cutting was more than just a business strategy. It was a tool of control, a way to tighten their hold on companies and ensure their dominance in the global market.

Dangerous Additives: The Hidden Harm in Everyday Products

In a bustling cityscape, where the hum of life never ceases, the average consumer is often unaware of the intricate web of decisions that influence their daily choices. From the cereal they eat in the morning to the soft drink they grab during lunch, there's a hidden narrative, a story of corporate manipulation and profit-driven motives. And at the heart of this narrative is BlackStone.

It was a rainy afternoon when investigative journalist, Clara Mitchell, stumbled upon a confidential document in her mailbox. The envelope was unmarked, but its contents were explosive. It detailed a series of advisories from BlackStone to various food and beverage companies, pushing them to incorporate specific chemicals into their products. These chemicals, while enhancing flavor and addictiveness, had known health risks.

Clara's eyes widened as she read through the list. Some of these additives were linked to serious health conditions, from heart diseases to cognitive impairments. But what was even more shocking was the rationale behind their inclusion: increased consumer loyalty and, consequently, higher profits.

Determined to expose this, Clara arranged a covert meeting with Dr. Alex Rutherford, a renowned food scientist. In a dimly lit café, they pored over the document. "It's all here," Dr. Rutherford whispered, his fingers trembling. "These chemicals, especially when combined, can be incredibly harmful. But they're also addictive. They ensure that once a consumer starts, they keep coming back for more."

Clara leaned in, "But why would BlackStone push for this? Surely, they understand the implications?"

Dr. Rutherford sighed, "It's not about the consumer's well-being. It's about the bottom line. If a product is addictive, it guarantees repeat sales. And in the corporate world, that's gold."

The two of them delved deeper, uncovering a series of covert meetings between BlackStone advisors and top executives from major food corporations. In one such meeting, held in a luxurious penthouse overlooking the city, BlackStone's lead advisor, Marcus DeLorenzo, was captured on a hidden microphone saying, "It's simple economics. Give the people what they crave, and they'll empty their pockets for you. Health concerns? Those are long-term. We're focused on the now."

As the story broke, there was public outrage. Protests erupted outside BlackStone's headquarters, with people demanding accountability. But amidst the chaos, the corporate giant remained eerily silent, shielded by their vast influence and power.

This chapter serves as a chilling reminder of the lengths to which corporations, under advisories like those from BlackStone, might go. It's a tale of profits over people, where consumer health is sacrificed at the altar of corporate greed.

The Health Implications: A Vicious Cycle of Dependency

In a sprawling metropolis, hospitals and clinics were seeing an unprecedented surge in patients. From young children to the elderly, a myriad of health issues were on the rise. Dr. Lydia Hartman, a seasoned physician, couldn't help but notice the pattern. The ailments her patients presented with were eerily similar: respiratory problems, heart conditions, and a spike in diabetes. But what was the root cause?

One evening, as Dr. Hartman sat in her office sifting through patient records, she was interrupted by a knock on the door. It was her old friend, investigative journalist Clara Mitchell. "Lydia," Clara began, her voice tinged with urgency, "I've been digging into BlackStone's advisories to food companies. They're pushing for additives that are not just addictive but harmful."

Dr. Hartman's eyes widened in realization. "That's it! The additives in the food products are leading to these health issues. It's a direct correlation."

But the rabbit hole went deeper. As the two women collaborated, they discovered another sinister layer to BlackStone's strategy. Not only were they advising food companies, but they also had significant investments in the pharmaceutical industry. It was a diabolical plan: first, create a health crisis through harmful food products, and then profit from the treatments and medications required to address those very health issues.

In a dimly lit bar, Clara met with an insider from BlackStone, a whistleblower who agreed to speak on the condition of anonymity. "It's all interconnected," he confessed, taking a sip of his drink. "The more people get sick, the more they need medication. And guess who benefits from both ends? BlackStone."

He went on to describe secret board meetings where executives would toast to the "cycle of profitability." They would celebrate quarterly reports showing spikes in both food sales and pharmaceuticals. It was a win-win for them, but at the cost of public health.

Clara, with a determined glint in her eyes, asked, "How deep does this go? How many companies are involved?"

The whistleblower hesitated, then whispered, "Almost all of them. From the snacks in your pantry to the pills in your medicine cabinet, BlackStone has its fingerprints everywhere."

The revelation was staggering. The very institutions people trusted to safeguard their health were the ones compromising it. And at the center of this web was BlackStone, orchestrating a vicious cycle of dependency.

As news of this broke, there was a global outcry. Health organizations called for immediate investigations, and consumers demanded transparency. But amidst the uproar, BlackStone remained a formidable force, shielded by its vast empire and influence.

This chapter serves as a stark reminder of the lengths to which corporate giants can go in their relentless pursuit of profit. It's a tale of manipulation and deceit, where the health of millions is traded for the enrichment of a few.

Eroding Industry Integrity: The Broader Impact of BlackStone's Advisories

In the bustling heart of New York City, a group of industry leaders gathered for their annual summit. The atmosphere was tense, a stark contrast to the usual camaraderie. The topic on everyone's lips was BlackStone's pervasive influence and the erosion of trust it had caused.

At a corner table, two CEOs, Richard Thompson of Thompson Foods and Elena Martinez of PureLife Organics, engaged in a hushed conversation. "It's not just about profits anymore, Elena," Richard lamented, swirling his drink. "BlackStone's advisories have made us question the very essence of our industry. How did we let it come to this?"

Elena sighed, "We were blinded by the promise of increased revenues. But now, our consumers doubt the authenticity of our products. It's a PR nightmare."

Across the room, a group of young entrepreneurs, pioneers of the 'clean and green' movement, discussed the challenges they faced. "Every time we try to introduce a genuinely organic product, we're undercut by these giants who've compromised on quality due to BlackStone's advisories," said Maya, the founder of GreenBite. "It's hard to compete when the playing field is so skewed."

As the evening wore on, whispers of regulatory capture began to circulate. Journalist Alex Reid, known for his investigative pieces, shared his findings with a select few. "BlackStone's reach isn't limited to corporations," he revealed. "There's evidence to suggest they've influenced regulatory bodies, ensuring their advisories face minimal scrutiny."

A hush fell over the group as the implications of Alex's words sank in. If regulatory bodies were compromised, where did that leave the consumer? The very institutions designed to protect them were now in question.

In a private suite upstairs, Lara Simmons, a former BlackStone executive turned whistleblower, met with a few trusted allies. "It's a web of deceit," she confessed. "BlackStone's advisories aren't just about maximizing profits. They're about control. By eroding the integrity of industries, they create a void, a void they're all too eager to fill."

The revelations of the night were damning. Industries, once revered, were now under the scanner. Brands that families had trusted for generations were now subjects of skepticism. And at the heart of this distrust was BlackStone, pulling the strings, orchestrating a grand puppet show.

As dawn approached, a resolve formed among the attendees. They would fight back, rebuild the trust, and reclaim the integrity of their industries. But the road ahead was long, and BlackStone's shadow loomed large. The battle for the soul of industry had just begun.

The Global Implications: A World Under BlackStone's Thumb

In the bustling markets of Delhi, street vendors hawked their wares, unaware that many of the products they sold were influenced by a corporation oceans away. Mothers, trying to provide nutritious meals for their families, unknowingly purchased foods laced with additives, a direct result of BlackStone's advisories to maximize shelf life and addictiveness.

Meanwhile, in a café in Paris, a group of economists discussed the alarming rise in obesity and diabetes rates. "It's not just France," remarked Pierre, a health economist, "It's a global trend. From Asia to Africa, we're seeing the same patterns. And the common thread? Companies under BlackStone's influence."

Across the Atlantic, in a boardroom in New York, BlackStone executives reviewed data charts showcasing their global influence. "Our advisories have been implemented in over 70% of the world's major corporations," boasted Gregory, a senior advisor. "From food to pharmaceuticals, our footprint is everywhere."

His colleague, Vanessa, chimed in, "And the beauty of it? As health deteriorates due to the products of companies we advise, our investments in the healthcare sector soar. It's a win-win."

In a university in Tokyo, Professor Akira Suzuki, a renowned global economist, lectured his students on the recent economic shifts. "We're witnessing a new form of colonialism," he began. "BlackStone, through its advisories, has created dependencies. Countries are now reliant on their products, their healthcare solutions, and even their financial systems. It's a global web of control."

Back in Africa, in a small village in Kenya, local farmers struggled to compete with cheap, mass-produced crops, a result of BlackStone's agricultural advisories promoting genetically modified seeds and intensive farming. Traditional farming methods were dying out, and with them, centuries of knowledge.

In Brazil, environmental activists protested against rapid deforestation, a consequence of BlackStone's advisories pushing for aggressive land use for agriculture and mining. The Amazon, the lungs of the Earth, was under threat, and with it, the planet's delicate ecological balance.

As the sun set over the horizon, casting a golden hue over the world, it became evident that this was not just about corporate profits. It was about control, dominance, and reshaping the world in BlackStone's image. From the food on our plates to the air we breathed, BlackStone's shadow loomed large, a puppet master in a global theater, with the strings of the world firmly in its grasp.

Conclusion: The Ultimate Game of Global Dominance

In a dimly lit, opulent boardroom at BlackStone's headquarters, a group of the company's top strategists gathered around a massive table made of mahogany. The walls were adorned with maps, charts, and graphs, each detailing the company's influence in various sectors around the world.

James, a senior strategist with silver hair and sharp features, leaned forward, his fingers steepled. "Gentlemen and ladies," he began, his voice dripping with confidence, "we've successfully embedded ourselves into the very fabric of global commerce. Our advisories, while seemingly benign, have allowed us to weave a web of influence that spans continents."

A younger executive, Clara, with a reputation for her ruthless efficiency, projected a world map on the screen. "Look at this," she said, pointing to the myriad of interconnected lines crisscrossing countries and continents. "Every line represents a company, an industry, a government that dances to our tune. From the food people eat in Africa to the cars they drive in Europe, our fingerprints are everywhere."

Ricardo, a suave strategist known for his expertise in emerging markets, chimed in, "It's not just about profits anymore. It's about control. By influencing corporate decisions, we're shaping societies, molding consumer behaviors, and even dictating political outcomes."

The room was silent for a moment, the weight of their influence palpable. Then, Helena, a veteran in the group with a penchant for philosophy, spoke up. "It's like a game of chess," she mused. "But instead of controlling mere pieces on a board, we're orchestrating global events. Every move, every advisory, is calculated, ensuring that the world bends to our will."

James nodded in agreement. "And the beauty of it? The world remains oblivious. They see the profits, the corporate successes, but they fail to see the strings being pulled behind the scenes."

Clara smirked, "And as they continue their daily lives, buying products, trusting brands, and consuming media, they're unknowingly playing into our hands, furthering our ultimate goal of global dominance."

As the meeting drew to a close, the executives left the room, each with a sense of accomplishment. They were not just business leaders; they were puppeteers in the grandest show on Earth. And as the world continued to spin, one thing was clear: BlackStone's game of global dominance was only just beginning.

Chapter 9
The Health Chain: Profiting from Sickness

Introduction: The Sinister Cycle of Health Exploitation

The bustling city of New York, with its towering skyscrapers and endless streams of people, was home to many secrets. One of its most closely guarded was nestled on the top floor of the BlackStone building, where a group of the company's elite met in a secluded conference room. The room, with its panoramic views of the city, was a testament to the company's vast reach and influence.

As the sun set, casting a golden hue over the city, Eleanor, BlackStone's Vice President of Health Initiatives, stood up to address the room. "Ladies and gentlemen," she began, her voice echoing with authority, "we are on the brink of revolutionizing the health industry. But not in the way the world expects."

She clicked a button, and a series of slides appeared on the screen behind her. Images of fast-food chains, sugary drinks, and processed foods filled the room. "We've successfully integrated ourselves into the very fabric of people's daily lives, ensuring that they consume products that, over time, deteriorate their health."

A murmur of agreement spread across the room. Eleanor continued, "But that's just the beginning. As these health issues arise, we position ourselves as the saviors." Another slide showcased a range of pharmaceuticals, health supplements, and private hospitals—all under BlackStone's umbrella.

Martin, a shrewd executive known for his analytical skills, interjected, "It's a masterstroke. We create the problem and then sell the solution. The profits are endless."

Eleanor nodded, "Exactly. And the world remains blissfully unaware. They see us as champions of health, investing in cutting-edge medical research and solutions. Little do they know, we're the puppeteers behind their health crises."

A young analyst, Sophia, raised her hand hesitantly. "But isn't this ethically questionable?" she asked, her voice quivering slightly.

Eleanor fixed her with a cold stare. "Ethics is a luxury in our line of business. Our goal is dominance, and we'll achieve it by any means necessary."

The room fell silent, the gravity of their actions weighing heavily. They were not just manipulating markets or industries; they were playing with the very lives of people. And as the night deepened, the city below remained oblivious to the sinister cycle of health exploitation orchestrated from above.

The Food Industry: Crafting the Health Crisis

In a lavish penthouse overlooking the heart of Manhattan, a private dinner was underway. The guest list was exclusive, comprising CEOs of major food corporations, renowned chefs, and influential food critics. At the head of the long, ornate table sat Victor Hale, BlackStone's Director of Food and Beverage Initiatives.

Raising his glass for a toast, Victor began, "To a future where our brands dominate every household's dining table!" The room erupted in cheers, the clinking of glasses echoing the sentiment.

As the evening progressed, Victor unveiled BlackStone's latest advisory for the food industry. "Our research indicates," he began, pulling up a series of charts, "that certain additives increase the addictive quality of foods. By incorporating these into your products, we can ensure repeat customers and skyrocketing sales."

A CEO from a leading soda company leaned forward, intrigued. "Are these additives safe?"

Victor smirked, "Safe enough to pass regulations. And with our influence over regulatory bodies, we can ensure minimal scrutiny."

A renowned chef, known for his popular chain of fast-food restaurants, chimed in, "But won't we face backlash for compromising on health?"

Victor responded confidently, "That's the beauty of it. We'll launch a series of health campaigns promoting exercise and balanced diets. The public will be too busy blaming themselves to question the food they consume."

As the night wore on, deals were struck, and strategies were formulated. Recipes were altered, with unhealthy additives discreetly making their way into everyday foods. From sugary cereals targeting children to processed meals for adults, no stone was left unturned.

Sophia, the young analyst from the previous meeting, found herself at this dinner, observing the proceedings with growing horror. She discreetly approached Clara, a journalist known for her investigative pieces on the food industry. "The world needs to know about this," Sophia whispered, handing Clara a flash drive containing all of BlackStone's advisories.

Clara nodded, her eyes filled with determination. "Trust me, they will."

As the dawn approached, the food industry was set on a dangerous path, with BlackStone pulling the strings. Unbeknownst to them, however, seeds of resistance were being sown, setting the stage for an epic showdown between corporate greed and the public's right to know.

The Rise of Lifestyle Diseases: A Predictable Outcome

In the bustling city of New York, Dr. Amelia Hartman, a seasoned cardiologist, was witnessing an alarming trend. Her clinic, once frequented by elderly patients, was now seeing an influx of younger individuals, many in their 30s and 40s, presenting with heart conditions typically reserved for those decades older.

One afternoon, as she reviewed the medical history of a 35-year-old patient named Jake, she couldn't help but express her concern. "Jake, your cholesterol levels are off the charts. Have there been any significant changes in your diet recently?"

Jake hesitated, "Well, I've been consuming these new energy drinks. They're marketed as health boosters, and I thought they'd help with my long work hours."

Dr. Hartman sighed, "I've seen a spike in patients with similar stories. These products might promise health benefits, but they're loaded with sugars and harmful additives."

Meanwhile, at a local school, gym teacher Ms. Lydia noticed her students tiring more quickly during physical activities. Conversations with parents revealed a pattern: children were consuming processed snacks and sugary beverages at an alarming rate, products that had recently flooded the market.

One evening, at a community health seminar, Dr. Hartman and Ms. Lydia found themselves sharing their observations. They were approached by Clara, the investigative journalist. "I've been researching BlackStone's influence on the food industry," Clara whispered, "and I believe there's a direct link between their advisories and the health crisis we're witnessing."

The trio decided to collaborate, pooling their resources and expertise. Dr. Hartman began conducting surveys, revealing a staggering correlation between the consumption of BlackStone-influenced products and the rise in lifestyle diseases. Ms. Lydia organized awareness campaigns in schools, educating parents and children about the dangers lurking in their favorite snacks. Clara, armed with this data, wrote a series of explosive articles, exposing BlackStone's sinister role in the health epidemic.

As the stories gained traction, public outrage grew. Protests erupted outside BlackStone's headquarters, with people demanding accountability. Talk show hosts invited health experts, discussing the implications of corporate greed on public health.

In a dimly lit boardroom, BlackStone executives watched the chaos unfold. Victor, the Director of Food and Beverage Initiatives, remarked with a smirk, "Every crisis presents an opportunity. It's time to invest in the pharmaceutical sector."

The stage was set for BlackStone's next move, further entrenching their grip on the health chain. But with growing public awareness and a united front against their tactics, the battle was far from over.

The Pharmaceutical Goldmine: Profiting from Pain

In the heart of London, nestled among the city's iconic skyscrapers, stood the headquarters of MedPharmCo, one of the world's leading pharmaceutical companies. Its sleek glass facade reflected the city's hustle and bustle, but inside, the atmosphere was one of calculated calm. MedPharmCo had recently become one of BlackStone's most prized acquisitions, and the company's trajectory was about to take a sharp turn.

In the expansive conference room, BlackStone's senior executive, Richard Harlow, met with Dr. Elena Mitchell, MedPharmCo's Chief Research Scientist. The room, adorned with modern art and a panoramic view of the Thames, was a testament to the company's success.

"Dr. Mitchell," began Richard, leaning forward, "we've noticed a surge in lifestyle diseases globally. Diabetes, heart conditions, obesity... the list goes on. There's a massive market waiting to be tapped."

Dr. Mitchell, a woman of integrity and decades of experience, replied cautiously, "Indeed, Mr. Harlow. But our primary focus has always been on genuine research and providing effective solutions."

Richard smiled, revealing a hint of impatience. "That's all well and good, but think bigger. Imagine a world where MedPharmCo not only provides treatments but also preventive medications. We could have consumers on our products for life."

In a quiet cafe across town, two former college friends, Sarah, a health journalist, and Liam, a whistleblower from within MedPharmCo, met for a clandestine conversation. Liam, visibly distressed, shared, "Sarah, BlackStone's influence is changing everything. They're pushing for the rapid development of drugs, cutting corners, and even influencing doctors to prescribe them."

Sarah, her eyes widening, realized the gravity of the situation. "So, they create the health crisis through their food advisories and then profit from it by selling the cure? It's diabolical!"

Liam nodded, "And there's more. They're planning a global marketing campaign, targeting vulnerable populations, making them believe they need these medications."

As months rolled by, MedPharmCo's new line of drugs flooded the market. Advertisements showcased happy families, attributing their health and happiness to BlackStone-backed medications. Doctors, under the influence of hefty incentives, began prescribing them at an alarming rate.

However, Sarah, armed with Liam's insider information, began publishing a series of articles exposing BlackStone's dual role in both the health crisis and its supposed solution. Her revelations sent shockwaves through the global community, leading to investigations and public debates.

In a televised interview, Sarah passionately argued, "It's a cycle of exploitation! They're profiting from pain, from sickness. We need to break free from this manipulative chain."

As the world grappled with the revelations, BlackStone's pharmaceutical goldmine began to show cracks. But with their vast resources and influence, the battle for transparency and justice was only just beginning.

Straining Public Health Systems: The Broader Socio-Economic Impact

In the bustling corridors of St. Mercy Hospital, Dr. Laura Simmons, a seasoned physician, found herself overwhelmed. The influx of patients with lifestyle diseases had surged dramatically over the past year. As she reviewed patient files, a pattern emerged: many were regular consumers of products from companies under BlackStone's advisories.

One evening, as Laura sat in the hospital's dimly lit break room, she was joined by her old friend, Martin, an economist specializing in public health financing. Their conversations often revolved around the intersection of health and economics, but tonight, the tone was graver.

"Martin," Laura began, "we're swamped. The number of patients with preventable diseases is skyrocketing. And the worst part? Many can't afford the treatments."

Martin sighed, "It's not just here, Laura. Hospitals across the country are feeling the strain. And it's not just about the health implications. The economic burden is immense. With BlackStone's influence on both the food and pharmaceutical industries, they've created a perfect storm."

Laura took a sip of her coffee, "It's a double whammy. First, they profit from products that contribute to these health issues, and then they cash in on the treatments."

Martin nodded, pulling out a graph on his tablet. "Look at this. Health insurance premiums have shot up. The public health system is bleeding funds. And guess who benefits? Private insurance companies, many of which have ties to BlackStone."

Laura's eyes widened, "So, they're not just profiting from sickness, they're also capitalizing on the solutions?"

"Exactly," Martin replied. "And there's more. With strained public health systems, many are turning to private care, which is significantly more expensive. This widens the socio-economic gap. Those who can't afford private care are left with subpar treatment or, worse, no treatment at all."

In a downtown bar, two journalists, Aiden, and Priya, were piecing together a story on BlackStone's health chain influence. Aiden, looking pensive, said, "Priya, this isn't just about health. It's about social justice. The rich get richer, the poor get sicker, and the middle class is squeezed dry."

Priya nodded, "We need to expose this. The world needs to see the broader socio-economic implications of BlackStone's actions."

As the weeks rolled by, protests erupted worldwide. People demanded transparency, accountability, and a revamp of public health policies. Governments were forced to re-evaluate their ties with corporations, and the conversation shifted from mere health to the very fabric of society.

In the shadows, BlackStone's executives watched the unfolding events. Their vast empire was under scrutiny, and the world was waking up to the broader socio-economic impact of their actions. The battle for health, equity, and justice had begun.

Manipulating Medical Research and Drug Pricing: Controlling the Narrative

In the hallowed halls of the prestigious Langford Medical Research Institute, Dr. Helena Carter, a leading researcher in cardiology, was on the brink of a breakthrough. Her team had been investigating the long-term effects of certain food additives on heart health. The preliminary results were alarming, suggesting a direct link between these additives and heart diseases. But as she prepared to publish her findings, she faced unexpected resistance.

One evening, as Helena was working late, she was visited by Dr. Richard Grayson, the institute's director. Richard, a tall man with silver hair and piercing blue eyes, had an air of authority that was hard to ignore. "Helena," he began, choosing his words carefully, "I've reviewed your latest research. It's...controversial."

Helena looked up, surprised. "But the data is clear, Richard. These additives are harmful."

Richard sighed, "It's not that simple. Our institute receives significant funding from various corporations, some of which are under BlackStone's advisories. They've expressed concerns about your findings."

Helena's eyes widened in disbelief. "Are you saying we're being silenced?"

Richard hesitated, "It's more nuanced than that. BlackStone has a significant say in the medical research community. They fund studies, conferences, and even dictate the direction of certain research agendas. Your findings, while valid, threaten a narrative they've carefully crafted."

Meanwhile, in a posh restaurant downtown, two pharmaceutical executives, Alex and Isabelle, were discussing drug pricing strategies. Alex, swirling his wine, remarked, "Isabelle, our new heart medication is revolutionary. But we need to price it right."

Isabelle, with a sly smile, replied, "BlackStone's advisories have given us a clear direction. We can price it at a premium. With their influence over medical research, they've ensured that alternative treatments don't get the spotlight. Our drug will be in high demand."

Alex raised his glass, "To controlling the narrative."

Back at the institute, Helena was grappling with a moral dilemma. She confided in her colleague, Dr. Raj Patel. "Raj, our research could save lives. But we're being muzzled."

Raj, looking thoughtful, said, "Helena, BlackStone's reach is vast. They not only influence drug pricing but also the very research that determines medical best practices. It's a well-oiled machine."

Helena, determination in her eyes, responded, "Then we need to expose this. The world needs to know how medical research and drug pricing are manipulated for profit."

As the days turned into weeks, Helena and Raj began gathering evidence, reaching out to journalists, and building a case. The medical community was abuzz with whispers of a looming expose. The stage was set for a showdown between truth and power, science and profit, with the health of millions hanging in the balance.

Conclusion: The Dark Symphony of Health Exploitation

In a dimly lit room, high above the bustling streets of New York City, a group of BlackStone's top executives gathered around a mahogany table. The room, adorned with expensive art and a grand chandelier, exuded an air of opulence. At the head of the table sat Larry Lysander, the enigmatic CEO of BlackStone, his fingers tented, deep in thought.

"Colleagues," Larry began, his voice smooth and confident, "we've crafted a symphony within the health sector. A symphony that plays to our tune, where every note, every crescendo, is meticulously orchestrated."

A young executive, Clara, leaned forward, her eyes filled with admiration. "It's genius, really. We've not only influenced the food industry to create products that lead to health issues but also positioned ourselves to profit from the resulting medical needs."

Larry smiled, "Exactly, Clara. It's a cycle where we control both the cause and the cure. The public remains oblivious, believing they're making choices, when in reality, we're the puppeteers pulling the strings."

Across town, in a cozy bookstore, two investigative journalists, Marco and Lena, were piecing together the puzzle. Lena, her brow furrowed, said,

"It's like they're conducting a dark symphony, Marco. They've manipulated every aspect of the health chain."

Marco nodded, "From the food people eat to the drugs they take, BlackStone has ensured they profit at every stage. It's a masterclass in exploitation."

Lena sighed, "And the worst part? People trust these brands, these products. They believe they're making healthy choices, not realizing they're caught in BlackStone's web."

Back in the boardroom, Larry raised his glass for a toast. "To our continued success in the health chain. May we always stay one step ahead."

But as the night deepened, the winds of change were stirring. Marco and Lena's expose was about to hit the stands, threatening to disrupt BlackStone's dark symphony. The stage was set for a battle between corporate greed and the relentless pursuit of truth, with the health and well-being of millions hanging in the balance.

Chapter 10
The Political Weave: Manipulating the Strings of Power

Introduction: The Nexus of Business and Politics

In the heart of Washington D.C., a city known for its political power plays and monumental decisions, a clandestine meeting was taking place. The venue was an old, private club, its walls echoing with the whispers of deals and alliances forged over decades. Here, in a dimly lit room, two figures sat across from each other: Senator Richard Harlow, a veteran in the political game, and Larry Lysander, the charismatic heir to the BlackStone empire.

Adrian leaned back, swirling the amber liquid in his glass, his eyes never leaving the Senator's. "Richard," he began with a sly smile, "you and I both know the dance between politics and business. It's a delicate ballet, and BlackStone has always been keen to lead."

Senator Harlow, not one to be easily intimidated, responded, "Adrian, your family's influence in the political sphere is well-known. But remember, it's a two-way street. While you may have the capital, we hold the keys to the kingdom."

Adrian chuckled, "Ah, but that's where you're mistaken. Money doesn't just buy influence; it crafts policy, molds public opinion, and, if used wisely, can even shape the destiny of nations."

The Senator leaned in, intrigued. "What are you proposing?"

Adrian, with a glint in his eye, replied, "A partnership, Senator. BlackStone's resources and your political clout can achieve wonders. Together, we can redefine the global landscape."

Outside the club, a young journalist named Maya, tipped off about the meeting, tried to catch snippets of the conversation. She knew that the alliance between BlackStone and powerful political figures was more than just rumors. It was a nexus that had the potential to shift global dynamics.

As the evening wore on, the two men delved deeper into their plans, discussing trade agreements, regulatory changes, and even potential political appointments. It was clear that BlackStone's tentacles were not just limited to the corporate world; they were deeply entrenched in the corridors of power.

This was the world where business and politics intertwined, where decisions made behind closed doors impacted millions. And at the center of it all was BlackStone, masterfully weaving its web, always ensuring it remained at the pinnacle of power.

The Biden Administration: A Strategic Alliance

In the bustling heart of Washington D.C., the Biden administration was in full swing, setting the tone for a new era of American politics. The Oval Office, a symbol of power and prestige, was abuzz with activity. Advisors, diplomats, and key figures moved in and out, each playing their part in the intricate dance of governance. But amidst the sea of faces, there was one that stood out, not for his political stature, but for his corporate influence: Larry Lysander, the CEO of BlackStone.

One evening, as the sun set over the White House, Adrian found himself in a private meeting with President Biden. The room was filled with the soft glow of golden lamps, casting long shadows on the walls adorned with portraits of past presidents.

"Mr. Lysander," began President Biden, his voice firm yet cordial, "I've heard much about BlackStone's interests, especially in the energy and environmental sectors. What brings you here today?"

Adrian, ever the smooth operator, leaned forward, "Mr. President, BlackStone recognizes the challenges our planet faces. We believe in a sustainable future, and we're here to offer our expertise and resources to help shape America's environmental strategies."

Biden raised an eyebrow, "And in return?"

Adrian smiled, revealing a hint of his true intentions, "A seat at the table, Mr. President. An opportunity to influence policies that align with our vision."

As the conversation deepened, it became evident that BlackStone's involvement wasn't just about environmental strategies. They had their sights on a range of policy areas, from trade agreements to infrastructure projects. Their influence was pervasive, and they were adept at positioning themselves as invaluable allies.

Outside the White House, a group of environmental activists gathered, protesting against corporate influence in politics. Among them was Maya, the young journalist. Holding up her sign, she couldn't help but wonder about the true nature of the alliance between BlackStone and the Biden administration. Was it genuinely for the greater good, or was there a more sinister motive at play?

Back inside, as the meeting concluded, Adrian handed President Biden a sealed envelope. "A proposal, Mr. President. I believe it will be mutually beneficial."

Biden took the envelope, weighing it in his hands, both literally and metaphorically. The alliance with BlackStone promised resources and expertise, but at what cost?

As Adrian left the Oval Office, he felt a surge of confidence. BlackStone's influence was growing, and with the Biden administration as a strategic ally, their path to global dominance seemed all but assured.

Beyond Borders: BlackStone's Global Political Footprint

In the grand halls of London's Westminster, the chime of Big Ben echoed, signaling the start of another parliamentary session. As MPs gathered, there was an undercurrent of anticipation. Rumors had spread about a significant investment coming to the UK, and whispers of BlackStone's involvement were rife.

Across the channel, in the ornate chambers of the Élysée Palace in Paris, President Laurent Duval sat in a confidential meeting with his finance minister. "BlackStone has shown interest in our infrastructure projects," the minister began, "They're offering substantial funding, but they want certain... concessions."

Meanwhile, in the bustling metropolis of Tokyo, a high-profile gala was underway. Japan's elite had gathered, and amidst them was Larry Lysander, rubbing shoulders with politicians and business magnates alike. As he raised a toast, he subtly mentioned BlackStone's interest in Japan's tech industry, catching the ear of several influential figures.

From the vibrant streets of New Delhi to the historic squares of Rome, BlackStone's presence was palpable. Their strategy was clear: to embed themselves in the political fabric of nations, ensuring they had a say in policy decisions that would shape the future.

In a dimly lit private club in Berlin, a clandestine meeting took place. European leaders, away from the prying eyes of the media, discussed the continent's future. "BlackStone has been very generous with their donations to our campaigns," remarked a senator from Spain, sipping his aged whiskey. Another leader from Italy chimed in, "They've been advising us on our economic policies. Their insights have been... invaluable."

Back in New York, in BlackStone's opulent headquarters, a war room of sorts had been set up. Maps covered the walls, dotted with pins representing their global political connections. Analysts scurried about, tracking election results, policy changes, and political shifts. At the head of the table sat Adrian, overseeing this vast web of influence.

A young intern, fresh out of college, couldn't help but ask, "Mr. Blackwood, why are we so involved in global politics? Isn't our primary focus business?"

Adrian looked at him, a sly smile forming, "Business, my boy, is politics. And politics is power. By influencing policy discussions worldwide, we ensure BlackStone's interests remain not just central, but paramount."

As nations debated policies and charted their futures, behind the scenes, BlackStone's tendrils were ever-reaching, weaving a tapestry of control and dominance, ensuring that in the grand game of global politics, they were always several moves ahead.

Lobbying and Legislation: Shaping the Rules of the Game

In the heart of Washington D.C., nestled among historic buildings and monuments, lies K Street, the epicenter of lobbying in the United States. Here, in a lavish penthouse office with a panoramic view of the Capitol, BlackStone's lobbying team was hard at work. The walls were adorned with photos of senators, congressmen, and influential bureaucrats, all of whom had, at some point, been guests in that very room.

"Senator Mitchell's bill on environmental regulations is gaining traction," said Clara, the head lobbyist, as she reviewed a dossier. "If passed, it could hinder our oil ventures in the Gulf."

A younger lobbyist, Mark, chimed in, "I've scheduled a dinner with him next week. We've supported his campaigns in the past; it's time to call in a favor."

In another corner, a group was strategizing on an upcoming tax reform. "We need to ensure that the offshore provisions remain intact," said Robert, a seasoned lobbyist with ties to the Treasury. "I've got a meeting with the Secretary next Tuesday. I'll make sure our concerns are heard."

As days turned into nights, the team orchestrated a symphony of influence. Dinners, fundraisers, golf outings, and exclusive retreats were all tools in their arsenal. They knew the art of persuasion, and more importantly, they understood the value of reciprocity.

One evening, at an upscale D.C. restaurant, Clara sat across from a prominent congresswoman. "You know, Congresswoman, BlackStone has always admired your vision for this country," Clara began, pouring a glass of vintage wine. "This new regulation you're proposing, while noble, could have unintended consequences for businesses like ours."

The congresswoman looked thoughtful, taking a sip of her wine. "I'm open to discussion, Clara. Let's find a middle ground."

Back in New York, Larry Lysander received regular updates. He was particularly interested in a piece of legislation that could impact BlackStone's real estate ventures. "Ensure it doesn't see the light of day," he instructed, and his team knew they had their marching orders.

But it wasn't just in the U.S. BlackStone's influence extended to Brussels, where they lobbied European Union officials, and to capitals around the world, from London to New Delhi. Their goal was clear: to shape the rules of the game in their favor.

In a clandestine meeting in London, a British MP whispered to a BlackStone representative, "Your concerns about the new financial regulations have been noted. Consider it taken care of."

As the world watched, policies were crafted, and laws were passed. But behind the scenes, BlackStone's fingerprints were everywhere, subtly molding the world to fit their vision, ensuring that the rules of the game always favored their relentless pursuit of power and profit.

Diplomacy and Geopolitics: The Global Chessboard

In the opulent halls of international summits, where world leaders gathered to discuss the fate of nations, BlackStone was never far from the action. Their influence wasn't overt; you wouldn't see their logo emblazoned on banners or hear their name in speeches. Instead, their power was more insidious, operating in the shadows, whispered in hushed tones during closed-door meetings.

At a G20 summit in Buenos Aires, as leaders from the world's major economies convened, Larry Lysander, the enigmatic head of BlackStone, was seen in quiet conversation with several heads of state. To an onlooker, it might have seemed like casual chatter, but those in the know understood the weight of these discussions.

In a dimly lit private suite at the summit's venue, Adrian met with the Russian Foreign Minister. "Our investments in Siberia have been facing some... regulatory challenges," Adrian began, his voice smooth yet firm. "We were hoping Moscow could facilitate a smoother process."

The Foreign Minister, sipping his vodka, replied with a sly smile, "And what does BlackStone offer in return?"

Adrian leaned in, "Support for the Nord Stream project, perhaps? We have significant sway in certain European capitals."

In another part of the world, BlackStone's interests were shaping military decisions. A confidential report had revealed a vast untapped oil reserve in a disputed region between two African nations. BlackStone had significant stakes in exploration companies poised to benefit from this discovery. As tensions escalated between the two nations, diplomats from major powers intervened, but not just for peace. Behind the scenes, BlackStone's representatives were ensuring that any resolution favored their oil interests.

Trade agreements, too, bore the mark of BlackStone's influence. In Asia, as two economic giants negotiated a historic trade pact, BlackStone's interests were front and center. They had significant investments in industries that stood to gain immensely from reduced tariffs and eased regulations. And they made sure that the final agreement reflected this.

A European diplomat, speaking off the record at a private gathering in Geneva, remarked, "It's astonishing how BlackStone's interests align with so many diplomatic initiatives. It's as if they have a seat at the table, even if it's invisible."

And indeed, they did. From influencing decisions about sanctions on rogue nations (where, incidentally, BlackStone had business interests) to shaping the outcomes of climate accords based on their stakes in renewable energy, BlackStone was playing a high-stakes game on the global chessboard.

In the corridors of power, from Washington to Beijing, from Brussels to New Delhi, BlackStone's whispers were heard, their interests prioritized. They weren't just passive observers in the realm of geopolitics; they were puppeteers, pulling the strings of power, ensuring that the world danced to their tune.

Ethical Implications: Democracy at a Crossroads

In the heart of a bustling city, a dimly lit café became the rendezvous point for two old friends, both seasoned journalists, who hadn't seen each other in years. As they sipped their coffees, the conversation inevitably turned to the omnipresent influence of BlackStone.

"You know, Sarah," began James, adjusting his glasses, "I've been covering politics for over three decades, and I've never seen anything like this. It's as if our democratic institutions are being overshadowed by a single corporate entity."

Sarah nodded, her expression grave. "It's not just about lobbying or campaign donations anymore. BlackStone's reach has penetrated the very fabric of our democratic processes. When policy decisions are influenced more by corporate interests than by the will of the people, can we even call it a democracy anymore?"

James leaned in, lowering his voice, "I've heard whispers from my sources in the Capitol. Apparently, some of our elected representatives are more worried about BlackStone's stance on issues than their constituents'. It's like they're the unofficial 51st state."

Sarah sighed, "And it's not just here. Look at developing nations where BlackStone has significant investments. Leaders are more inclined to cater to BlackStone's interests than to address the pressing needs of their people. Poverty, education, healthcare – all take a backseat."

James interjected, "Remember that water crisis in Africa? BlackStone had stakes in a company that wanted to privatize the water supply. And suddenly, the government was pushing for privatization despite public outcry. It's as if the sovereignty of nations is up for sale."

Sarah looked pensive. "But it's not just about BlackStone's actions. It's about the ethical implications for our society. If a corporation can wield this much influence, what does it say about our values? About the principles our democracies were built upon?"

James nodded, "The lines between corporate and national interests are becoming so blurred. It's a dangerous precedent. Today it's BlackStone; tomorrow, it could be another entity. We're at a crossroads, and the very essence of democracy is at stake."

Sarah took a deep breath, "We need to shed light on this, James. People need to understand the magnitude of what's happening."

James agreed, "Absolutely. It's our duty as journalists. The world needs to recognize the threat BlackStone poses to democratic values and the sovereignty of nations. It's time to challenge this corporate behemoth and reclaim our democracies."

Conclusion: The Unyielding Grip on Power

In a grand hall adorned with opulent chandeliers and gilded frames, the world's most influential leaders gathered for an annual summit. Among them, a select few were privy to the silent puppeteer orchestrating many of the decisions made in that very room: BlackStone.

As the evening progressed, a hushed conversation took place in a secluded corner. Senator Mitchell, a veteran in politics, spoke with a young journalist named Clara, known for her fearless exposés. "You know, Clara," Mitchell began, his voice tinged with a mix of admiration and concern, "BlackStone isn't just another corporation. Their influence is unparalleled. They've managed to weave themselves into the very fabric of our political systems."

Clara, ever the inquisitive reporter, probed, "But Senator, how did it come to this? How did one entity gain such a stronghold?"

Mitchell sighed, taking a moment to choose his words. "It's a combination of strategic alliances, immense financial power, and an uncanny ability to always be several steps ahead. They've positioned themselves not just as advisors, but as indispensable partners to many in power."

A nearby ambassador, overhearing their conversation, chimed in, "It's not just in the U.S. In my country, BlackStone has been instrumental in shaping major policy decisions. They've become so embedded that it's hard to tell where their influence ends and genuine governance begins."

Clara's eyes widened, realizing the gravity of the situation. "So, they're essentially redefining the democratic process?"

Senator Mitchell nodded gravely. "Exactly. The democratic ideals we hold dear—of the people, by the people, for the people—are under threat. BlackStone's ambition isn't just about profit; it's about control, influence, and reshaping the world order to their liking."

The ambassador added, "And the worst part? They operate in the shadows, making it difficult to hold them accountable. Their grip on power is unyielding, and nations are struggling to maintain their autonomy."

Clara, ever determined, clenched her fist. "Then it's up to us, the fourth estate, to shine a light on their machinations. The world needs to understand the depth of BlackStone's infiltration."

Senator Mitchell smiled, a glint of hope in his eyes. "You're right, Clara. It's a daunting task, but if anyone can do it, it's you and your peers. The world needs to wake up to BlackStone's dark ambition that threatens our democratic ideals and the very autonomy of our nations."

Chapter 11
The Non-Profit Nexus: Benevolence or Ulterior Motives?

At first glance, BlackStone's association with major non-profits, such as the Gates Foundation, paints a picture of corporate responsibility and philanthropy. However, as with many of their endeavors, there's more than meets the eye. This chapter delves into the intricate relationships BlackStone has fostered within the non-profit sector, revealing a calculated strategy to further their global ambitions under the guise of benevolence.

In a sprawling, modern conference room, the board members of the Gates Foundation convened for their quarterly meeting. Among the attendees was a representative from BlackStone, Adrian, a suave, silver-haired man known for his persuasive charm. As discussions about new initiatives and partnerships began, Adrian's presence was felt, subtly steering conversations in directions favorable to BlackStone's interests.

Linda, a long-standing board member of the Foundation, whispered to her colleague, Dr. Raj, "Have you noticed how much influence Adrian seems to have in these meetings? It's as if BlackStone's interests are becoming intertwined with our mission."

Dr. Raj, a renowned epidemiologist, nodded in agreement. "Yes, and it's concerning. Just last week, I heard that a significant research grant we were about to award was redirected to another project that BlackStone has stakes in."

Linda raised an eyebrow, "You mean the malaria vaccine project?"

Dr. Raj sighed, "Exactly. While it's a worthy cause, there were other projects with more immediate impact that were sidelined. It's as if

BlackStone is using our foundation's reputation and reach to further their own agenda."

Meanwhile, Adrian was deep in conversation with another board member, discussing the potential of a new partnership in Africa. "Think of the possibilities," Adrian enthused, "By combining our resources, we can not only address critical health issues but also open up new markets for BlackStone's ventures."

As the meeting adjourned, Linda and Dr. Raj exchanged a worried glance. They both recognized the potential dangers of BlackStone's growing influence within the non-profit sector. While on the surface, their involvement seemed like a noble endeavor, the underlying motives were becoming increasingly apparent.

Outside the conference room, Adrian made a call. "The meeting went as expected," he reported, a sly smile playing on his lips. "The Gates Foundation is just the beginning. With our influence in the non-profit world, BlackStone will be unstoppable."

Back in her office, Linda pondered the implications. BlackStone's association with major non-profits wasn't just about philanthropy; it was a strategic move to infiltrate and influence global agendas. By aligning with powerhouses like the Gates Foundation, they could shape public opinion, dictate research directions, and even control vast resources meant for public good. The question that haunted her was: How could they ensure that benevolence remained the primary focus, and not become overshadowed by BlackStone's ulterior motives?

1. Strategic Philanthropy

In the opulent penthouse suite of BlackStone's headquarters, a group of executives gathered around a polished mahogany table. Charts, graphs, and reports were spread out, but the focus of the meeting wasn't on quarterly profits or stock prices. Instead, it was on a list of non-profits and charitable organizations.

"Let's talk strategy," began Helena, BlackStone's Vice President of Strategic Philanthropy. She was a sharp, astute woman with a reputation for turning every charitable act into a business opportunity. "Our next move is with the Whitmore Health Research Institute. They're on the brink of a breakthrough in diabetes research."

Across the table, Martin, the head of BlackStone's pharmaceutical division, leaned forward with interest. "And how does this concern us?"

Helena smirked, "Well, it just so happens that we've recently acquired significant shares in MedTech Labs, which is developing a new diabetes drug. If we fund Whitmore's research, they'll likely use MedTech's drug for their trials."

A murmur of appreciation went around the room. It was a classic BlackStone move—using philanthropy as a strategic tool to further their business interests.

James, a younger executive, looked puzzled. "But isn't that a conflict of interest? Funding research that directly benefits our investments?"

Helena laughed softly, "James, in the world of strategic philanthropy, it's all about leveraging assets. We're not just writing checks out of the goodness of our hearts. Every donation, every grant, every partnership is a calculated move. It's a win-win. The non-profits get their funding, and we get... well, let's just say a return on our investment."

Martin chimed in, "And let's not forget the positive PR. The public sees us donating millions to health research, and our image gets a nice little boost."

James still seemed uneasy. "But what if someone connects the dots? Realizes that our 'generosity' is just a cover for furthering our business agenda?"

Helena leaned back, a confident smile playing on her lips. "That's the beauty of it. It's all perfectly legal. And even if someone did raise a fuss, by the time any negative press comes out, we'll have moved on to our next strategic partnership."

As the meeting continued, the executives discussed other potential non-profit partnerships, each tied to a different arm of BlackStone's vast empire. From environmental organizations that could bolster their green initiatives to educational grants that would ensure a future workforce trained to their specifications, every charitable act was meticulously planned to serve BlackStone's broader goals.

Outside the towering skyscraper, the city buzzed with life, oblivious to the machinations happening within. But for BlackStone, every move, even in the realm of philanthropy, was a calculated step in their relentless pursuit of global dominance.

2. Access to Global Networks

In the dimly lit private dining room of an upscale restaurant, a clandestine meeting was taking place. At the head of the table sat Victor, BlackStone's Director of Global Expansion, a man known for his uncanny ability to open doors in the most challenging markets. Across from him was Dr. Aisha Nwosu, the charismatic founder of "Hope for Tomorrow," a non-profit dedicated to improving education and infrastructure in several African nations.

"Dr. Nwosu," Victor began, swirling his wine glass, "I've always admired the work your organization does. The schools you've built, the communities you've uplifted—it's truly commendable."

Aisha smiled politely, her eyes sharp. "Thank you, Mr. Victor. But let's cut to the chase. What does BlackStone want with a non-profit like ours?"

Victor chuckled, "Always straight to the point, I see. Very well. BlackStone believes in the power of partnerships. We've observed that 'Hope for Tomorrow' has an impressive reach in regions we're interested in."

Aisha raised an eyebrow, "And what regions might those be?"

"Let's take Nigeria, for instance," Victor replied, leaning forward. "Your organization has built schools, clinics, and even small-scale industries there. You have the trust of the local communities, relationships with policymakers, and an understanding of the socio-economic landscape. BlackStone sees immense potential in Nigeria, but we need a way in— a trusted partner who can help navigate the complexities."

Aisha took a sip of her drink, processing his words. "So, you want to use our non-profit as a gateway for your business ventures?"

Victor spread his hands, "Think of it as a mutually beneficial arrangement. BlackStone can provide funding, resources, and expertise to scale up your projects. In return, we gain access to local networks, insights into the market, and potential business opportunities."

Aisha leaned back, her expression thoughtful. "And what happens when BlackStone's interests clash with the needs of the communities we serve?"

Victor smiled, revealing a hint of the predator beneath the polished exterior. "Dr. Nwosu, in the world of business and philanthropy, there's always a way to align interests. We just need to find the right balance."

As the evening wore on, the two engaged in a dance of negotiation, each trying to gauge the other's intentions. For BlackStone, non-profits like "Hope for Tomorrow" were more than just charitable organizations—they were gateways to untapped markets, political influence, and global dominance. And they were willing to do whatever it took to ensure their place at the top.

3. Reputation Management

In the heart of New York City, BlackStone's towering headquarters stood as a testament to their financial prowess. But as with any empire, maintaining a pristine image was crucial. Inside one of the building's opulent conference rooms, a team of PR experts, led by the charismatic Isabelle Hart, convened for a strategy session.

"Alright, team," Isabelle began, her voice commanding the room's attention. "We've had a few PR hiccups recently, especially with our investments in the fossil fuel sector and some questionable land acquisitions in South America. We need a game-changer, something that will shift the narrative."

A young executive, Lucas, cleared his throat, "What about increasing our association with major non-profits? Organizations like the Gates Foundation or Save the Children?"

Isabelle's eyes lit up. "Exactly. Associating with such respected entities can help us cultivate a positive public image. It's the perfect smokescreen."

Another executive, Maria, chimed in, "We could sponsor major events, set up joint initiatives, or even launch a global campaign addressing issues like hunger or education. The media loves a good philanthropy story."

Isabelle nodded, "And while they're busy covering our charitable endeavors, they'll be less inclined to dig into our more... controversial activities."

Lucas, ever the strategist, added, "Moreover, these non-profits have a vast following. By aligning with them, we not only divert attention from our contentious investments but also tap into a broader audience, further solidifying our reputation."

A murmur of agreement spread across the room. However, a more seasoned executive, Mr. Grayson, raised a valid concern. "But what happens when these non-profits discover our ulterior motives? They have their own reputation to uphold."

Isabelle smirked, "That's where our negotiation skills come into play. We offer them something they can't refuse—funding, resources, access to our global networks. In the world of non-profits, resources are always scarce. They'll find it hard to turn down our offers, especially if it means furthering their cause."

The room was silent for a moment, each individual absorbing the gravity of the strategy. It was a masterful play—using benevolence as a shield, all while furthering BlackStone's global ambitions. The meeting concluded with a sense of renewed purpose, as the team set forth to weave their web of influence, one non-profit at a time.

4. Influence on Policy and Regulation

In the dimly lit private dining room of an upscale restaurant in Washington D.C., a clandestine meeting was underway. At the head of the table sat Victor Kane, BlackStone's Chief Strategy Officer, a man known for his uncanny ability to navigate the murky waters of politics and business. Opposite him was Dr. Eleanor Mitchell, the influential head of a prominent non-profit organization advocating for global health reforms.

"Dr. Mitchell," Victor began, swirling the wine in his glass, "Your organization has done commendable work in the field of global health. Your recent campaigns have garnered significant attention, and policymakers are listening."

Eleanor nodded, her eyes sharp. "Thank you, Mr. Kane. We believe in making a tangible difference. But as you know, advocacy requires resources, and resources are finite."

Victor smiled, sensing an opportunity. "That's precisely why I wanted to meet you. BlackStone is keen on supporting initiatives that align with our vision. We believe that by collaborating, we can achieve mutual benefits."

Eleanor raised an eyebrow, intrigued yet cautious. "Go on."

Victor leaned in, "Your organization has a strong voice in policy circles. We've noticed your push for certain health reforms, some of which intersect with our interests. BlackStone is willing to provide significant funding and resources to your campaigns. In return, we'd appreciate a seat at the table when these policies are being drafted."

Eleanor hesitated, weighing the implications. "You're asking for influence over our policy recommendations."

Victor nodded, "Influence, Dr. Mitchell, but not control. Think of it as a partnership. Your organization gets the resources it needs, and BlackStone ensures that the policies, while beneficial to the public, also align with our long-term objectives."

The room was thick with tension. Eleanor took a deep breath, "I'll need to discuss this with my board. But I won't deny that the resources you're offering could significantly amplify our impact."

Victor smiled, sensing a potential alliance. "Take your time, Dr. Mitchell. BlackStone is patient. We understand the value of strategic partnerships."

As the evening wore on, the two delved deeper into potential collaborations, laying the groundwork for a partnership that would intertwine the worlds of non-profit advocacy and corporate ambition. The lines between benevolence and ulterior motives were becoming increasingly blurred, and BlackStone was once again positioning itself to pull the strings from behind the curtain.

5. Data Collection

In a sprawling, state-of-the-art data center located in an undisclosed location, rows upon rows of servers hummed with activity. This was BlackStone's data hub, a place where information from various sources converged, giving the company an unparalleled edge in its operations.

A young data scientist named Clara was hard at work, analyzing the latest batch of data that had just been uploaded. This wasn't just any data; it was a comprehensive health report from a non-profit operating in Sub-Saharan Africa. The report detailed the spread of a new strain of malaria, its impact on local communities, and the efforts being made to combat it.

As Clara sifted through the data, she noticed patterns and trends that could be of interest to BlackStone's pharmaceutical investments. She quickly drafted a report and headed to the office of Adrian Wolfe, BlackStone's Head of Data Analytics.

Knocking lightly, she entered the spacious office. "Adrian, you need to see this," she said, handing over her report.

Adrian skimmed through the pages, his eyes widening with realization. "This is gold, Clara. If this strain spreads at the predicted rate, there'll be a massive demand for a new vaccine. And guess what? One of our pharmaceutical companies is in the early stages of developing one."

Clara nodded, "Exactly. With this data, they can tailor their research, expedite trials, and be the first to market. The potential profits are astronomical."

Adrian leaned back in his chair, a sly smile forming on his lips. "And all thanks to our 'benevolent' partnership with that non-profit. Who would've thought that charity could be so... lucrative?"

The two shared a knowing look. For BlackStone, every piece of data was a potential goldmine, a puzzle piece in their grand scheme of global dominance. And by aligning with non-profits, they had tapped into a treasure trove of information, all under the noble guise of philanthropy. The world saw them as benefactors, but in the shadows, they were strategists, always ten steps ahead, always plotting, always profiting.

In a dimly lit, upscale restaurant in New York City, two figures sat across from each other, their faces illuminated only by the soft glow of candlelight. One was Larry Lysander, the CEO of BlackStone, and the other was Dr. Elise Mitchell, the head of a prominent environmental non-profit.

Their conversation was hushed, their tones measured. "Elise," began Larry, swirling his wine glass, "I've always admired the work your organization does. Protecting the environment, raising awareness—it's all very noble."

Elise smiled politely, her eyes sharp. "Thank you, Larry. But let's cut to the chase. Why did BlackStone donate such a significant sum to our organization?"

Larry leaned in, his voice dripping with charm. "Consider it a gesture of goodwill. We believe in your cause. But, as you know, we're heavily invested in the new hydroelectric project in South America. There's been some... opposition to it, citing environmental concerns."

Elise's eyes narrowed. "You mean the dam that'll displace thousands and flood a significant portion of the rainforest? Our organization has been vocal about its potential harm."

Larry nodded. "Yes, that's the one. But think of the bigger picture, Elise. The energy it'll provide, the jobs it'll create. And with your organization's endorsement, the project could move forward without any hitches."

Elise took a deep breath, processing his words. "You're asking us to compromise our values, Larry."

He leaned back, a sly grin on his face. "I'm asking for a partnership. Think of the resources we could provide the projects we could fund together. All I ask is for a more... favorable stance on this one project."

The weight of the decision pressed down on Elise. Aligning with BlackStone could bring unparalleled resources to her organization, but at what cost? The integrity of her non-profit was at stake.

This was just one of many instances where BlackStone's deep pockets and strategic donations raised eyebrows. Throughout this chapter, readers will be taken on a journey, uncovering the intricate web of influence, money, and power. From health initiatives in Africa to educational programs in Asia, BlackStone's fingerprints were everywhere, always ensuring their interests were safeguarded, even if it meant swaying the very organizations built on integrity and altruism.

In conclusion, in a world where corporate social responsibility is often lauded, BlackStone's philanthropic endeavors could easily be mistaken as genuine acts of goodwill. On the surface, their generous donations to non-profits and their partnerships with charitable organizations paint a picture of a corporation with a heart, one that understands its role in the larger societal framework and is eager to give back.

However, as one delves deeper into the maze of their charitable activities, a different narrative begins to emerge. At the heart of this narrative is a meticulously crafted strategy, one that is less about benevolence and more about control. Each donation, each partnership, and each initiative is a calculated move on the global chessboard, designed to further BlackStone's interests.

Take, for instance, a gala event held in a grand ballroom adorned with crystal chandeliers and golden drapes. The event, organized by a renowned non-profit, was attended by the who's who of the business and political world. As the evening progressed, a representative from BlackStone took to the stage, announcing a multi-million dollar donation to the non-profit. The room erupted in applause, but in a quiet corner, two attendees exchanged a knowing glance. "Yet another investment in their global portfolio," one whispered to the other.

Indeed, for BlackStone, these acts of 'charity' are investments. Investments that allow them access to influential figures, that enable them to shape policies, and that provide them with a shield against any criticism. After all, how could a company so generous, so involved in bettering the world, be questioned?

But those who have watched BlackStone's rise know better. They understand that in the grand theater of global dominance, every act, no matter how noble it appears, has an ulterior motive. And for BlackStone, that motive is clear: to weave an unbreakable web of influence, ensuring that they remain puppeteers, pulling the strings of power from behind the curtain.

In the end, BlackStone's dance with the non-profit sector is a masterclass in manipulation. It's a reminder that in the quest for power, even acts of kindness can be weaponized. And as the world applauds their generosity, BlackStone inches closer to their ultimate goal: a world where their dominion is unchallenged and absolute.

Chapter 12
The Global Resonance: The Final Note in BlackStone's Symphony of Control

The sun was setting over the sprawling metropolis, casting long shadows over the towering skyscrapers. In a penthouse suite, high above the city, a group of BlackStone's top executives gathered around a polished mahogany table. The room was filled with the soft hum of conversation, punctuated by the clinking of glasses. The view from the windows was breathtaking, but the real spectacle was unfolding inside.

"Look at this," said one executive, spreading out a map on the table. The map was dotted with red pins, each representing a point of BlackStone's influence. "From the tech hubs of Silicon Valley to the oil fields of the Middle East, from the bustling markets of Asia to the financial centers of Europe, we are everywhere."

Another executive chimed in, "It's not just about geographical presence. Think about the sectors. Energy, media, health, politics, non-profits... there's no domain untouched by our influence."

A third added, "And it's not just about control. It's about resonance. Every move we make, every decision, sends ripples across the globe. And the world, knowingly or unknowingly, dances to our tune."

As the evening wore on, stories were shared - tales of political maneuverings, corporate takeovers, and strategic alliances. There was the story of a small town mayor who had opposed a BlackStone project, only to find himself out of office after a sudden scandal. There was the tale of a journalist who had tried to expose BlackStone's unethical practices, only to be discredited and shunned by his peers. And then there was the account of a rival corporation that had tried to challenge BlackStone's dominance, only to find itself facing a series of inexplicable setbacks.

As the stories flowed, a pattern emerged. BlackStone wasn't just a corporation; it was a force, a behemoth that shaped the world in its image. Its influence was so pervasive that it was almost invisible, like the air we breathe. And those who dared to oppose it found themselves facing an adversary that was everywhere and nowhere at the same time.

The evening drew to a close, and as the executives left the penthouse, they looked out at the city below, a vast expanse of lights and shadows. It was a world they had helped shape, a world that moved to the rhythm of BlackStone.

In this final chapter, as we reflect on the vast empire that BlackStone has built, we are left with a chilling realization. Their influence is not just about control; it's about resonance. Every decision they make, every move they orchestrate, sends ripples across the globe. And in this symphony of control, BlackStone is the conductor, and the world is their orchestra. The question that remains is: are we, the people, mere instruments in their grand performance, or do we have the power to change the tune?

1. **The Global Chessboard**

   The room was dimly lit, the only source of light emanating from a massive holographic projection of the world map. Around it stood a group of BlackStone's elite strategists, their eyes scanning the glowing continents, each marked with symbols representing BlackStone's assets and influence.

   "Look at Africa," murmured one strategist, pointing towards the continent illuminated with several glowing nodes. "Our investments in the mining sector there have given us unparalleled control over the global supply of rare earth metals."

   Another strategist, her fingers dancing over a tablet, brought up a detailed view of Europe. "And here, our influence in the financial hubs of London and Frankfurt allows us to sway economic policies, ensuring they align with our long-term objectives."

A third, older gentleman, leaned forward, his fingers tracing the trade routes in the South China Sea. "Our partnerships in the shipping industry here mean we control a significant portion of global trade. We're not just participants; we're puppeteers."

The conversation shifted to South America, where BlackStone's interests in agriculture and energy sectors were shaping regional politics. Then to the Middle East, where their stakes in oil and infrastructure projects were influencing geopolitical dynamics.

As the hours passed, the discussion became more animated. The strategists played out various scenarios, predicting how political elections, economic downturns, or even natural disasters could be turned to BlackStone's advantage. It was like watching grandmasters play a game of chess, but the stakes were much higher. This was a game that spanned continents, cultures, and economies.

One of the younger strategists, a recent recruit, looked overwhelmed. "How do we keep track of it all?" he asked. "The world is so complex, so unpredictable."

The oldest strategist, who had been with BlackStone for decades, smiled wryly. "That's the beauty of it," he said. "We don't just react to the world; we shape it. We've positioned ourselves in such a way that no matter what happens, we benefit. It's not about predicting the future; it's about creating it."

The meeting concluded with a sense of satisfaction. BlackStone wasn't just a player on the global stage; they were the stage itself. Every major event, every shift in power, every trend could be traced back to their influence. And as they continued to weave their web of control, the world danced, knowingly or unknowingly, to their tune.

2. The Illusion of Choice

In a lavish penthouse overlooking the city's skyline, a group of BlackStone's top executives gathered around a mahogany table. The room was filled with the soft hum of conversation, punctuated by the clinking of crystal glasses filled with the finest wines. On the walls, screens displayed real-time data, tracking everything from stock market fluctuations to trending social media topics.

"Have you seen the latest sales figures for our beverage division?" one executive, a sharply dressed woman named Clara, asked with a smirk. "Our new energy drink is flying off the shelves."

A younger executive, Mark, nodded in agreement. "It's incredible. And to think, just a few months ago, that same product was struggling. All it took was a few well-placed endorsements and a viral marketing campaign."

Clara leaned in, her voice dropping to a conspiratorial whisper. "And let's not forget the slight tweak in the recipe. A little more sugar, a little more caffeine, and voila! Instant addiction."

The group laughed, but their amusement wasn't just about the success of a product. It was the realization of the power they wielded. The ability to shape consumer preferences, to make people crave something they didn't even know they wanted.

Across the room, another group was discussing politics. "I still can't believe we managed to get our candidate elected," mused Robert, a seasoned political strategist. "The odds were against us."

His colleague, a silver-haired man named Victor, chuckled. "It's all about perception, my friend. We control the media, we control the narrative. People thought they were making a choice, but in reality, we were the puppet masters, pulling the strings."

Robert raised his glass in a toast. "To the illusion of choice."

Victor nodded, his eyes cold and calculating. "It's the most powerful tool in our arsenal. Give people the semblance of freedom, make them believe they're in control, and they'll never suspect the truth."

As the night wore on, the discussions ranged from business to politics, from culture to technology. But the underlying theme was always the same: control. BlackStone had mastered the art of manipulation, creating a world where every choice, every decision, was influenced by their desires. And the most terrifying part? Most people had no idea they were dancing to BlackStone's tune.

3. Economic Dominance

In the heart of London's financial district, the atmosphere inside BlackStone's European headquarters was electric. The trading floor was a hive of activity, with brokers shouting orders, screens flashing with numbers, and the constant ringing of phones. But above this chaos, in a soundproofed room with a panoramic view of the city, sat BlackStone's economic strategists, the real puppeteers behind the global economy.

Liam, a seasoned economist with a reputation for his uncanny ability to predict market movements, leaned back in his chair, observing the floor below. "You know, it's almost poetic," he mused. "All these people, thinking they're in control, when in reality, it's us pulling the strings."

His colleague, Isabelle, a brilliant data scientist who had developed BlackStone's proprietary trading algorithms, nodded in agreement. "It's all about data and patterns. With the amount of information we have, we can predict, with astonishing accuracy, how markets will move. And with that knowledge, we can influence them."

Liam smirked, "Remember the Asian financial crisis in the late '90s? Or the more recent cryptocurrency crash? All it took was a little nudge from us, a strategic sale here, a rumor there, and the dominos began to fall."

Isabelle sipped her coffee, her eyes gleaming with mischief. "And the best part? While the world scrambles to pick up the pieces, we're already ten steps ahead, capitalizing on the chaos."

A third member of their team, Raj, who specialized in emerging markets, chimed in, "It's not just about making money. It's about control. By having a stranglehold on key sectors of the economy, we can influence national policies, sway elections, and even determine the fate of entire nations."

Liam nodded, "Exactly. When a country's economy is in turmoil, they come to us, hat in hand, looking for a bailout. And in return, we get to dictate the terms, ensuring our interests are always protected."

Isabelle looked out of the window, her gaze distant. "We're not just a company; we're an empire. And the world is our playground."

The trio shared a knowing look, fully aware of the immense power they wielded. Through their economic dominance, BlackStone had become more than just a corporate entity. They were a force of nature, shaping the destiny of the global economy and, by extension, the lives of billions.

4. Narrative Control

In a dimly lit room, a group of BlackStone's top communication strategists gathered around a large mahogany table. The walls were adorned with screens displaying news channels from around the world. At the head of the table sat Eleanor, BlackStone's Chief Communications Officer, known in inner circles as the "Narrative Weaver."

"Alright, team," Eleanor began, her voice commanding attention. "Our influence over the media landscape is unparalleled. But we must always be vigilant. The narrative is a delicate thing, and it's our job to shape it."

A young strategist named Marcus piped up, "The recent partnership with the European news conglomerate has given us a significant foothold in the region. Their networks reach over 200 million viewers daily."

Eleanor nodded, "Excellent. And with our existing control over major US and Asian outlets, we're essentially shaping the global conversation. But it's not just about controlling the news. It's about influencing the influencers."

A woman named Clara, who headed the social media division, added, "We've successfully placed our assets in key influencer positions across platforms. From YouTube to TikTok, our narratives are being subtly woven into popular culture. The younger generation, especially, is consuming content that aligns with our objectives, often without even realizing it."

Eleanor smiled, "That's the beauty of it. When the message is everywhere, it becomes the truth. But we must also be prepared to quell dissenting voices."

A man named Alejandro, who was in charge of BlackStone's online surveillance unit, responded, "We've developed algorithms that can identify and suppress content that goes against our narrative. Any blogger, vlogger, or independent journalist that tries to expose our influence is quickly discredited or drowned out."

Marcus chimed in, "And let's not forget our 'think tanks' and 'research institutions.' They provide the intellectual backing to our narratives, giving them an air of credibility. When a renowned scholar or expert speaks, people listen."

Eleanor leaned back, her eyes scanning the room. "We're not just telling a story; we're crafting reality. And in this reality, BlackStone's vision is the only one that matters."

The room was silent, each member fully aware of the gravity of their role. They were not just spin doctors or PR experts; they were architects of perception, molding the very fabric of global consciousness to suit BlackStone's grand design.

5. The Shadow Government

In the heart of Washington D.C., Senator Mitchell sat in his opulent office, staring at the emblem of BlackStone engraved on a gold-plated card. The card was an invitation to an exclusive event, one that would be attended by the world's most influential leaders, both in the public eye and behind the scenes.

His aide, a young woman named Jessica, noticed his contemplative expression. "Another invitation from BlackStone, sir?"

Mitchell sighed, "Yes. They're everywhere, aren't they? From the halls of Congress to the boardrooms of Wall Street. It's as if they've woven themselves into the very fabric of our governance."

Jessica hesitated before speaking, "I've heard rumors, sir. Whispers in the corridors. They say that BlackStone has its own council, a sort of 'shadow government' that pulls the strings from behind the curtain."

Mitchell leaned back in his chair, "I've heard those whispers too. And the scary part? I believe them. I've seen firsthand how they operate. They have their agents in every major political party, in every key committee. It's not just about campaign donations or lobbying. It's deeper than that. They have a vision for the world, and they're implementing it step by step."

Jessica looked concerned, "But why? What's their endgame?"

Mitchell looked out of the window, "Control. Absolute control. They want to shape the world in their image, and they have the resources and the patience to do it. Governments come and go, but BlackStone? They're here to stay."

Suddenly, his phone buzzed. It was a message from an unknown number: "Looking forward to seeing you at the event, Senator. - B."

Mitchell's face turned pale. "They're always watching, always listening. It's as if they're omnipresent."

Jessica whispered, "What do we do, sir?"

Mitchell took a deep breath, "We play the game, for now. But always remember, Jessica, while they might have the power, we have the people. And one day, the people will see BlackStone for what they truly are."

As the sun set over the capital, the two figures in the room were united in their resolve, aware of the monumental challenge that lay ahead. They knew that BlackStone's shadow loomed large, but they also believed in the power of democracy and the indomitable spirit of the people.

6. The Endgame

In a dimly lit room, high above the city skyline, two figures sat across from each other, a vast mahogany table between them. One was Mr. Larry Lysander, the CEO of BlackStone, and the other, a renowned journalist named Clara who had been granted a rare interview.

Clara, her voice steady but filled with curiosity, began, "Mr. Grayson, the world sees BlackStone as a financial behemoth, but rumors suggest there's more to the story. What is BlackStone's endgame?"

Grayson leaned back, his fingers steepled, eyes piercing as he studied Clara. "You're right," he began slowly, "Money is just a tool, a means to an end. Our vision is grander. We seek a world of order, a world where chaos is curbed, and predictability reigns."

Clara pressed on, "But at what cost? Your methods have been called manipulative, even sinister."

A sly smile crept onto Grayson's face. "History is written by the victors, Ms. Clara. Every empire, every great civilization, has had to make... choices. Choices that might seem harsh in the moment but are necessary for the greater good."

Clara leaned forward, "And who decides this 'greater good'? You? BlackStone?"

Grayson chuckled, "Not just us. But we do play a part. Think of it this way: in a world filled with noise, wouldn't you want someone to orchestrate a harmonious symphony? That's what we do. We ensure that the world functions in harmony, to a tune that benefits all."

"But it seems to benefit BlackStone the most," Clara retorted.

Grayson's gaze hardened, "We bear the burden of leadership. With great power comes great responsibility. And yes, we reap the rewards, but we also pave the way for progress, stability, and prosperity."

Clara took a deep breath, realizing the depth of BlackStone's ambition. "So, you want a world where BlackStone's word is law, where every decision, every narrative, is shaped by you?"

Grayson nodded, "A world where our interests safeguard the future. A world of order, Ms. Clara. And in that order, everyone has a place, everyone benefits."

The room grew silent as the weight of Grayson's words settled. Clara understood that BlackStone's vision was not just about dominance but reshaping the very fabric of society. The interview was over, but the story, Clara realized, was just beginning.

In Conclusion

In a world increasingly interconnected and interdependent, the melodies of power and control play out in the grand auditorium of global politics and economics. BlackStone, with its vast resources and unparalleled influence, has positioned itself as the lead conductor in this global orchestra. But as we've journeyed through the annals of their strategies and maneuvers, it's evident that their symphony is not one that seeks to unite, but rather to subjugate.

Imagine, if you will, a grand concert hall. The audience, representing the global populace, comes with the hope of witnessing a harmonious performance. Yet, as the curtain rises, it's BlackStone that takes center stage, wielding the conductor's baton with an iron grip. Each movement of their symphony, from media manipulation to political puppetry, is meticulously crafted to drown out any discordant notes.

In one poignant scene, a young activist named Lila stands up amidst the audience, trying to raise her voice against the overwhelming sound. "Can't you all hear it?" she cries out, her voice trembling but determined. "This isn't the music of unity or progress. It's a dirge of control and subjugation!"

Yet, her voice, like many others, is drowned out by the overpowering crescendo that BlackStone orchestrates. Their influence, as we've seen, isn't just about controlling markets or political agendas. It's about shaping perceptions, molding beliefs, and ultimately, determining the very course of our shared global destiny.

But as the final notes of their composition threaten to engulf the world in a singular, monotonous tune, there's a glimmer of hope. Whispers of dissent begin to emerge, growing louder and more persistent. From the corners of the world, voices rise in unison, challenging the maestro's dominance. It's a reminder that while BlackStone might be orchestrating the present, the future remains unwritten.

As we conclude this exploration, it's imperative for each of us to ask: Do we want to be mere spectators in this grand performance, or do we want to be co-composers of our global future? The power of BlackStone is undeniable, but history has shown that when the many unite, even the most formidable empires can be challenged. The final note in BlackStone's symphony of control is yet to be played, and it's up to us to ensure that it's one of hope, unity, and shared prosperity.